# ATHENS

| CONDENSED |

 victoria kyriakopoulos

LONELY PLANET PUBLICATIONS
Melbourne • Oakland • London • Paris

# contents

Athens Condensed
1st edition – May 2002

Published by
Lonely Planet Publications Pty Ltd
ABN 36 005 607 983
90 Maribyrnong St, Footscray, Vic 3011, Australia
**e** www.lonelyplanet.com or AOL keyword: lp

Lonely Planet offices
Australia Locked Bag 1, Footscray, Vic 3011
☎ 613 8379 8000  fax 613 8379 8111
**e** talk2us@lonelyplanet.com.au
USA   150 Linden St, Oakland, CA 94607
☎ 510 893 8555  Toll Free: 800 275 8555
fax 510 893 8572
**e** info@lonelyplanet.com
UK   10a Spring Place, London NW5 3BH
☎ 020 7428 4800  fax 020 7428 4828
**e** go@lonelyplanet.co.uk
France  1 rue du Dahomey, 75011 Paris
☎ 01 55 25 33 00  fax 01 55 25 33 01
**e** bip@lonelyplanet.fr
www.lonelyplanet.fr

Design Yvonne Bischofberger Maps Joelene Kowalski,
Charles Rawlings-Way & Cris Gibcus Editing Melanie
Dankel & Elizabeth Swan Cover James Hardy & Maria
Vallianos Publishing Manager Diana Saad Thanks to
Gabrielle Green, Rachel Imeson, Tony Davidson, Annie
Horner, Helen Papadimitriou, Quentin Frayne, Rowan
McKinnon, LPI & GIS Unit

Photographs
Many of the images in this guide are available for
licensing from Lonely Planet Images:
**e** www.lonelyplanetimages.com

Front cover photographs
Top: Looking through columns at the Parthenon
(Rick Gerharter)
Bottom: Fallen column at the Temple of Olympian Zeus
(Mark Honan)

ISBN 1 74059 350 2

Text & maps © Lonely Planet Publications Pty Ltd 2002
Photos © photographers as indicated 2002
Printed by The Bookmaker International Ltd
Printed in China

# how to use this book

## SYMBOLS

- ✉ address
- ☎ telephone number
- Ⓜ nearest metro station
- 🚉 nearest train station
- 🚌 nearest bus route
- 🚗 auto/taxi route
- ⊘ opening hours
- ⓘ tourist information
- Ⓢ cost, entry charge
- ⒠ email/website address
- ♿ wheelchair access
- ♟ child-friendly
- ✗ on-site or nearby eatery
- Ⓥ good vegetarian selection

## COLOUR-CODING

Each chapter has a different colour code which is reflected on the maps for quick reference (eg all Highlights are bright yellow on the maps).

## MAPS

The fold-out maps inside the front and back covers are numbered from 1 to 9. All sights and venues in the text have map references which indicate where to find them on the maps; eg (2, C3) means Map 2, grid reference C3. Although each item is not pin-pointed on the maps, the street address is always indicated.

## PRICES

Price gradings (eg €10/5) usually indicate adult/concession entry charges to a venue. Concession prices can include senior, student, member or coupon discounts.

## THE AUTHOR

**Victoria Kyriakopoulos**

Victoria first flirted with Athens in 1988 and snuck back for a few flings before moving there in mid-2000 for a full-blown affair. Her some-what irrational reaction to the city – and country – has bewildered many, not least her father and cat back in Mel-  bourne. A former staff writer with *The Bulletin*, columnist with *The Age*, and government press secretary, she is deputy editor of the Athens-based *Odyssey* magazine. She is also a freelance correspondent for *The Age* and other publications.

Thanks to: Mary Retiniotis, Chris Anastassiades, Vicky Valanos, Michael Howard and Angela Papalani.

## READER FEEDBACK

Things change – prices go up, schedules change, good places go bad and bad places improve or go bankrupt. So, if you find things better or worse, recently opened or long since closed, please tell us and help make the next edition even more accurate. Send all correspondence to the Lonely Planet office closest to you (listed on p. 2) or visit www.lonelyplanet.com/feedback/.

# facts about athens

Modern Athens was always going to have it tough living up to its past glory. Whatever it did, the Acropolis stood above the city, a reminder of its former brilliance in the arts, philosophy, architecture and politics.

While the city's history and ancient monuments hold endless fascination for visitors, the concrete sprawl beyond them often fails to inspire. Few fall in love with Athens at first sight. It's an acquired taste, but the chaos and contradictions of the city can be as seductive as they are frustrating.

Athens developed into a modern capital in less than 200 (often turbulent) years. Much of the phenomenal – and ugly – growth has happened in the past 50 years, which saw the city's population grow to 3.5 million.

And it is still a work in progress. Major changes taking place for the 2004 Olympics will consolidate an evolution that has taken a decade. The city's beautification, addition of green, open space and infrastructure improvements will make it a more efficient and modern city to be in.

Much of the appeal lies beyond the facade, a quirky pulse and energy, a communal angst counterbalanced by a zest for the good life.

Athens is a city of hedonists and consumers, modern philosophers, anarchists, fashion victims and ordinary people surviving in an evolving society. The pace can be fast (the public service aside) but people still take time out for a coffee. Athens is alive long after the rest of Europe has gone to bed – and there's certainly something oddly life-affirming about 3am traffic.

John Elk III

*The Acropolis at night taken from Filopappou Hill.*

# HISTORY
## Ancient Athens
The Acropolis drew some of Greece's earliest Neolithic settlers. By 1400BC, it had become a powerful Mycenaean city whose territory covered most of Attica. By the end of the 7th century BC, Athens had become the artistic centre of Greece.

Athens was ruled by aristocrats, generals and the *arhon* (chief magistrate) until the reform-oriented Solon, the harbinger of democracy, became arhon in 594BC and declared all free Athenians equal by law.

In 490BC, the Persian army reached Attica but suffered a humiliating defeat when outmanoeuvred in the Battle of Marathon. They invaded again in 480BC, and burned Athens to the ground.

## The Classical Age
Under Pericles' leadership (461-429BC), the treasury moved from Delos to Athens and an illustrious building program began. Athens experienced a golden age of unprecedented cultural, artistic and scientific achievement.

However Athens' expansionist ambitions eventually sparked the Peloponnesian Wars, in which Athens suffered badly. In the first war (431-421BC) plague broke out in the city, killing a third of the population, including Pericles. After Athens surrendered to Sparta in the second war, its fleet was confiscated, the Delian League abolished and the walls between the city and Piraeus torn down.

## Hellenistic Period
The northern kingdom of Macedon led by Philip II emerged as the new power in 338BC. After Philip's assassination, his son Alexander (the Great) became king and by the end of the 3rd century BC had spread Hellenism into Persia, Egypt and parts of India and Afghanistan.

## Roman Rule
Athens was defeated by Rome in 189BC after it backed an enemy of Rome in Asia Minor, but the city escaped lightly as the Romans had great respect for Athenian scholarship. After a second ill-fated rebellion, the Romans destroyed the city walls and carted off many of its finest statues to Rome.

For the next 300 years, Athens experienced an unprecedented period of peace – the Pax Romana – during which Roman emperors, particularly Hadrian, graced Athens with many grand buildings.

## Byzantine Empire
With the rise of the Byzantine Empire, which blended Hellenistic culture with Christianity, the capital of the Roman Empire was transferred to the Greek city of Byzantium, which was renamed Constantinople (present-day Istanbul) in AD330.

The Byzantine Empire outlived Rome, lasting until the Turks captured Constantinople in 1453. Christianity was made the official religion in Greece in 394, with the worship of 'pagan' Greek and Roman gods banned.

Athens remained an important cultural centre until 529, when the teaching of classical philosophy was forbidden in favour of Christian theology. From 1200-1450, Athens was occupied by a succession of opportunistic invaders – Franks, Catalans, Florentines and Venetians.

## Ottoman Rule

In 1456, Athens was captured by the Turks, who ruled Greece for the next 400 years. The Acropolis became the home of the Ottoman governor, the Parthenon was converted into a mosque and the Erechtheion was used as a harem.

*The Church of Holy Apostle (from the Byzantine period) is only a stone's throw from the Acropolis; see it on the walking tour detailed on p. 62.*

Turkish control of the city was interrupted briefly in 1687 when a Venetian general laid siege to the Acropolis for two months. It was during this campaign that the Parthenon was blown up when Venetian artillery struck gunpowder stored inside the temple.

## Independence

On 25 March 1821, the Greeks launched the War of Independence and on 13 January 1822 independence was declared. But infighting twice escalated into civil war, allowing the Ottomans to recapture Athens whereupon the Western powers stepped in and destroyed the Turkish-Egyptian fleet in the Bay of Navarino.

In April 1827, Ioannis Kapodistrias was elected president, and the city of Nafplion named the capital. After Kapodistrias was assassinated in 1831, Britain, France and Russia again intervened, declaring Greece a monarchy. To avoid taking sides, the throne was given to 17-year-old Prince Otho of Bavaria, who transferred his court to Athens, which became the capital in 1834.

At the time there were about 6000 residents in Athens. King Otho (as he became) brought in Bavarian architects to create a city of imposing neo-classical buildings, tree-lined boulevards, flower gardens and squares. Sadly, many of these building have been demolished.

## World War II & the Greek Civil War

Athens thrived and enjoyed a brief heyday as the 'Paris of the Eastern Mediterranean' before WWI. A disastrous Greek attempt to seize former Greek territories in southern Turkey, known as the Asia Minor catastrophe, ended with the Treaty of Lausanne in July 1923.

More than one million Greeks were forced out of Turkey in the ensuing population exchange. Many headed for Athens, virtually doubling the city's population overnight.

During the German occupation of the city in WWII, more Athenians were killed by starvation than by the enemy. After the war, fighting between communist and monarchist resistance groups led to a bitter civil war which ended in October 1949, leaving the country in a political, social and economic mess.

In a mass exodus, almost a million Greeks migrated to the USA, Canada and Australia. A mammoth reconstruction and industrialisation program in Athens prompted another population boom, as people from the islands and villages moved to the city.

## The Junta & Monarchy

In 1967, a group of right-wing army colonels (the junta) launched a military coup. In the ensuing seven-year reign, political parties and trade unions were banned and opponents were jailed or exiled.

On 17 November 1973, tanks stormed a student protest sit-in at Athens' Polytechnic, killing at least 20 students. The US-backed junta's downfall came after the disastrous attempt to topple the Makarios government in Cyprus provoked a Turkish invasion of the island.

Democracy returned to Greece in 1974 and a referendum subsequently abolished the monarchy, which remains in exile today (and in dispute with the government over assets). The left-wing PASOK government of Andreas Papandreou was elected in 1981, the same year Greece entered the European Union (EU).

## Athens Today

Since the 1980s, fundamental changes have taken place, the most dramatic in the past 10 years. Athens has a conspicuously wealthier society, although there are still major economic disparities and a rural-city divide.

Greece is fast becoming part of the global economy, with foreign companies making investments and a raft of privatisations bound to change the notorious public sector mentality and bureaucracy. Greece is also becoming a major economic player in the Balkans.

Authorities have embarked on an ambitious program to modernise the city, with key elements being the expansion of the road and metro networks, and the new international airport at Spata, east of Athens. Confidence is riding high and billions are being poured into city centre redevelopment.

# ATHENS 2004

In 1997, Greece won its bid to stage the Olympic Games – for the first time since the inaugural modern Olympics were held in Athens in 1896. The return of the Games to their birthplace will mark a major turning point for the country.

In the long term, the Olympics could prove the greatest gift for Greece – fast tracking long-overdue infrastructure improvements. In the short term, they present the greatest challenge – delivering an event of a scale the nation has never seen will exhaust all the country's resources.

While the Olympic Games date back to Mycenaean times, the first official record of the quadrennial games was in 776BC. Held in honour of Zeus, they took place at Olympia and were open to all Greek males. Later, the Romans were permitted to participate.

Beyond the athletic competition, the Olympics were a major cultural and social event; writers, poets and historians read their works to large audiences, leaders talked politics and traders did deals. During the Games, a truce was observed between warring parties.

The last Games were held in AD394 after they were banned as part of a purge of pagan festivals. They were revived by Frenchman Pierre de Coubertin, who believed in the power of sport to inspire the human spirit and encourage peace.

With the exception of the two world wars, the Games have been held every four years since 1896, growing at a gargantuan rate.

### The Stadium

Built in the 4th century BC for the Panathenaic contests, the Roman Stadium (7, M8) was rebuilt in Pentelic marble by Herodes Atticus and, after years of disuse, was restored for the first modern Olympics in 1896.

With marble seats for 70,000, the 'Kallimarmaron', as it is known, cannot meet the needs of the modern-day games, but is expected to play some sort of ceremonial role in 2004.

*It's a long way to the top if you wanna climb the Roman Stadium.*

*The Olympic spirit still burns in Athens.*

The return to Athens will coincide with the scaling down of the Games, universally acknowledged as having become over-commercial, extravagant and too big for most nations to host.

Greece is emphasising its historic ties to the Games and the original ideals, and is reviving the Olympic Truce as a mechanism for peace.

## ORIENTATION

Athens lies in a basin surrounded by hills which is bounded in the south by the Saronic Gulf. Several other hills dot the plain, the most famous being the Acropolis and the city's other major landmark – and highest point – Lykavittos Hill (277m).

*Not the best way to spend your day.*

Greece lies in one of most seismically active regions in the world. In 1999, an earthquake registering 5.9 on the Richter Scale struck Athens leaving 139 dead and 100,000 homeless, mostly in the outer northern suburbs.

The main city centre is concentrated around the triangle that goes from Syntagma to Omonia to Monastiraki. It's hard to get lost – the Acropolis and Lykavittos help you get your bearings.

## ENVIRONMENT

Athens' Mediterranean climate means hot, dry summers and mild winters with bright sunny days. In July and August, heatwaves can send the mercury soaring above 40°C (over 100°F) for days on end and the city can be unbearably hot. Warm summer nights force people out for relief, contributing to Athens' lively nightlife. It does not rain for months on end in the summer.

Greece is belatedly becoming environment-conscious, with campaigns being implemented in schools. An army of road-sweepers tackle the litter problem in the city, but rural areas can be a disgrace.

*Cleaning up the city.*

Athens suffers less now from the dreaded *nefos*, the blanket of smog that still covers the city on bad days. Restrictions on vehicles in the centre, better public transport, the gradual abolition of leaded petrol and tougher laws have reduced vehicle and industrial pollution.

Under a €117 million program to increase green space, more than one billion trees, shrubs and plants are to be planted in the Attica area by 2004. Although forest fires remain a major problem throughout Greece.

# GOVERNMENT & POLITICS

Since 1975, Greece has been a parliamentary republic with a president as head of state. The president and 300-member parliament have joint legislative power.

The ruling socialist Pasok party, led by Prime Minister Costas Simitis, has been in power for 17 years, apart from a brief comeback by the conservative New Democracy party in 1990-3. An election is due in early 2004, although the pundits suggest a change of government is unlikely so close to the Olympics (August 2004).

Athens is part of the prefecture (*nomos*) of Attica. Since being elected in 1995, Mayor Dimitris Avramopoulos, who is sometimes compared to New York's Rudy Guiliani, has launched a major program of public works and beautification of the city's streets, buildings and squares, which has revitalised the centre of town. Avramopoulos has formed his own political party and plans to run in the next election.

### The Diaspora

Greece maintains strong links with more than four million Greeks living around the world, including an estimated two million in the US and Canada. Many return for annual holidays, own property and are involved in the political and cultural life of the country of their birth (or their ancestors').

The Greek government has a significant commitment to promoting Greek language, culture and religion abroad and has established a dedicated General Secretariat for Greeks Abroad. Melbourne, Australia, has the 3rd-largest population of Greek-speakers in the world, after Athens and Thessaloniki.

# ECONOMY

Greece's entry to the European Monetary Union in January 2002 was a momentous achievement. The historic drachma was phased out from February 2002 to make way for the euro.

Tight fiscal policy, structural reforms and a comprehensive program of deregulation and privatisation of the telecommunication, electricity, shipping and airline industries in recent years have improved the country's economy. In 2001, the government was projecting a budget surplus for the first time in 30 years.

The Greek GDP has been growing by 3.5%, the 3rd-highest growth rate in the EU. Tourism is now the biggest industry, and the majority of the workforce is employed in services (68% of GDP) and industry (23.5%), with agriculture contributing only 8.5%.

Unemployment is still high but inflation is being contained after dropping from 20% in 1990 to 3.6% in late 2001. The last census estimated Athens population at 3.5 million, including more than 600,000 immigrants.

Overall, Greece's economic prospects have never looked brighter. A stock market frenzy in the late 1990s made a lot of people rich but many ordinary punters lost out in the ensuing crash, from which the Bourse is still recovering.

# SOCIETY & CULTURE

Although there are now Athenians of several generations standing, most residents today are relative newcomers to the city who migrated to Athens from other parts of Greece or from Greek communities around the world.

Many are descended from families forced out of the Smyrna (now Izmir) region of south-western Turkey in 1923 or arrived in the 1950s from rural areas of Greece during the country's comparitively belated entry into the industrial era.

**Did you Know?**
Population: 3.5 million
Inflation rate: 3.5%
Greek GDP per capita: US$12,652
Unemployment: 11.3%
Average house prices: €1750 per sq m
Number of tourists: 12.5 million
Average wages: €12,600 per annum

Many Athenians still retain a strong link to their village or island of origin, returning periodically to see parents and grandparents or using family properties as holiday homes.

Once a country of emigrants, Greece is again attracting large numbers of migrants, both legal and illegal, including a wave of Albanians and economic refugees from the Balkans, the former Soviet Union, Bangladesh, Iran and Iraq. Immigration is changing the social and economic landscape and forcing Greek society to confront new social issues.

Greece remains largely culturally homogenous and steeped in traditional customs. Name days (celebrating the saint after whom a person is named) are more important than birthdays and come with an open-house policy where you are expected to feed all well-wishers. Weddings and funerals are also events of great significance in Greek society. Greeks are superstitious and believe in the 'evil eye' (bad luck brought on by envy), so avoid being too complimentary about things of beauty, especially newborn babies.

About 98% of the Greek population belong to the Greek Orthodox Church. Most of the remainder are Roman Catholic, Jewish or Muslim. Religion remains an important criteria in defining what it is to be a Greek, as the recent debate over the removal of religion from the state-issued ID card proved. Furthermore, the Greek year is centred on the festivals of the church calendar.

**Do's & Don'ts**
The Greek reputation for hospitality is not a myth, just a bit harder to find these days in a big, self-absorbed city. Greeks are generous hosts, and guests are expected to contribute nothing to a meal or social gathering. If you are invited out for a meal, the bill is not shared – insisting can insult your host.

Personal questions are not considered rude in Greece, and queries about your age, salary, marital status are considered normal and opinions expressed freely.

The younger generations of Greeks are highly literate, often studying abroad, a high proportion speak English and are in tune with world trends, fashion and music.

# ARTS

The artistic legacy of ancient Greece remains unsurpassed, with enduring influence in Western civilisation. People still read Homer's *Iliad* and *Odyssey*, written in 9th century BC, and ancient sculptures take pride of place in the collections of the world's great museums. Generations of artists have been influenced by the ancient Greeks, from primitive and powerful forms of prehistoric art to the realism of the Hellenistic period that inspired Michelangelo.

*Aphrodite showing Pan who's boss at the National Archaeological Museum (p. 28).*

## Drama & Theatre

Drama dates back to the contests staged in Athens during the 6th century BC for the annual Dionysia festival. At one of these contests, Thespis left the ensemble and took centre stage for a solo performance – considered the first true dramatic performance and leading to the term 'thespian'.

A strong theatre tradition continues today, with the works of the ancient Greek playwrights such as Aeschylus, Sophocles, Euripides and Aristophanes performed in the few surviving ancient theatres during summer festivals.

## Literature

The pre-eminent ancient poets included Pindar, Sappho and Alcaeus. Modern celebrated poets include Constantine Cavafy and the two Nobel Prize laureates, George Seferis (1963) and Odysseus Elytis (1979).

The controversial Nikos Kazantzakis, author of *Zorba* and *The Last Temptation,* remains the most celebrated 20th-century Greek novelist. A spate of translations of modern Greek writers was showcased in October 2001 when Greece was the guest nation at the annual Frankfurt Book Fair.

## Music

Music has always been a feature of Greek life, but not many have made it big internationally, the notable exceptions being opera diva Maria Callas, living legend Mikis Theodorakis, Vangelis, Demis Roussos and Nana Mouskouri. A new generation of musicians, however, is starting to make an impact on the world music scene.

## Cinema

For many years Greek cinema has been characterised by esoteric, arthouse films, exemplified by the slow, visual feasts of Theodoros Angelopoulos, winner of the 1998 Cannes Palmes d'Or award for *An Eternity and One Day*. Greek cinema, long in the doldrums, is experiencing a revival after the domestic commercial success of a number of Greek films.

# ARCHITECTURE

The influence of ancient Greek architecture can be seen today in buildings from Washington, DC to Melbourne. Greek temples, seen throughout history as symbols of democracy, have been the inspiration for major architectural movements such as the Italian Renaissance and the British Greek Revival.

One of the earliest known examples of Greek architecture is the huge Minoan palace complex at Knossos on Crete.

In the Archaic and classical periods, monumental temples were characterised by Doric, Ionic and Corinthian columns – the Temple of Athena Nike and the Erechtheion on the Acropolis being two famous examples. The distinct and ornate Corinthian column features a single or double row of leafy scrolls, subsequently used by the Romans, notably on the Temple of Olympian Zeus.

During the Hellenistic period, private houses and palaces, rather than temples and public buildings, were the main focus.

Byzantine churches built throughout Greece usually featured a central dome supported by four arches on piers and flanked by vaults, with smaller domes at the four corners and three apses to the east. The external brickwork, which alternated with stone, was sometimes set in patterns.

After independence, Athens continued the neoclassical style that had been dominant in Western European architecture and sculpture, exemplified by the grandiose National Library and the Athens University.

Many neoclassical buildings were destroyed in the untamed modernisation that took place in the 1950s, 1960s and 1970s, when most of the ugly concrete apartment blocks that now characterise the modern city were built.

A number of old mansions are now museums and many more are being restored as buildings and have become heritage protected. The wonderful design of the new metro, with art and antiquities is in stark contrast to the bland German-designed airport that could be anywhere. Innovative restorations such as the old Gazi gasworks complex and the Athinais Centre, in an old silk factory, have been world class.

Spanish architect Santiago Calatrava has designed the 2004 Olympic complex, but is it hoped new Olympics-related projects allow the new generation of Greek architects to leave their own architectural legacy.

*Detail of the ancient Parthenon of Athens*

Neil Setchfield

# highlights

Ancient Athens was tiny compared to the sprawling metropolis of today. This makes it easy for visitors to see the historic centre, major landmarks and attractions; the rest of the city is a little more complex.

The highlights featured here are merely the pick of the bunch – there are many gems to be discovered just by walking around the city. As most of the important archaeological sites and museums are within walking distance of the centre (and each other), seeing the city on foot is the best option.

If you are visiting in summer, it is best to see the archaeological sites early in the morning and spend the hottest part of the day at a museum. Many sites and state-run museums close by 2pm – another reason to go early. On the other hand, heading to the Acropolis a little later might mean you avoid the tour groups. Make sure you wear good-soled shoes as the ancient marble surfaces can be very slippery and uneven.

## Stopping Over

**One Day** Head to the Acropolis, the crowning jewel of the city, and the Ancient Agora, then amble through Plaka's Anafiotika quarter and stop for lunch at a taverna. Walk through the Roman Agora and the Tower of the Winds before browsing through the Monastiraki Flea Market. Visit the Parliament and see the changing of the guards, before heading to the National Archaeological Museum. Spend the evening walking the streets of Plaka. Dine under the Acropolis or head to a Psirri bar or restaurant for some live music.

**Two Days** Go to the Museum of Cycladic Art and the Benaki Museum where you can lunch on the rooftop overlooking the National Gardens, then wander through Kolonaki's boutiques and cafes. Visit the Byzantine and Christian Museum. Catch a summer show at the Herodes Atticus Theatre or take the funicular railway up Lykavittos Hill for a panoramic view of Athens.

### lowlights

Things that can stress you out in Athens:

- Traffic, pollution, noise and Athens' drivers
- Footpaths that can be uneven, potholed and treacherous
- Having to yell to hail a speeding taxi in peak hour
- The small percentage of rip-off taxi drivers
- The early closing hrs of many sights
- Trying to master the new 10-digit telephone number system (p. 116)

Neil Setchfield

**Three Days** Visit the National Gallery of Art, stroll through the National Gardens and stop for a coffee at Aigli and walk over to the old Olympic Stadium and the Temple of Olympian Zeus. Head into Plaka for some souvenir shopping. Go to Piraeus' Mikrolimano port for a seafood dinner by the water and a drink at a swish bar.

# ACROPOLIS (7, L4)

Even when you live in Athens, the site of the Acropolis can still make your heart skip a beat. Time, war, pilfering, earthquakes and pollution have taken their toll on the sacred hill – and its crowning glory, the Parthenon (p. 18) – yet it stands defiant and dignified over Athens and remains the most important ancient monument in the Western world.

Many of the Acropolis' monuments have regrettably been stripped or destroyed over the years or put into museums, so there are many replicas in place. Major restoration work is attempting to stop the deterioration of the marble, which has suffered from industrial pollution and traffic fumes. The site is now World Heritage listed.

First inhabited in Neolithic times, it served as a fortress, a place of cult worship, and archaeologists believe there may have even been a Mycenaean palace on the peak. Many temples were built on Acropolis (High City) paying homage to the goddess Athena.

After the buildings were destroyed by the Persians in 480BC, Pericles began his ambitious building program which transformed the Acropolis into a magnificent city of temples. In subsequent years, the buildings were converted into Christian churches and mosques.

In 1687, the Venetians attacked the Turks and opened fire on the Acropolis causing a massive explosion (the Ottomans stored gunpowder in the Parthenon) which severely damaged the buildings.

Entry is through the **Beulé Gate and Monument**, named after the French archaeologist who uncovered it in 1852. Beyond it are the **Propylaia**, built in 437-432BC, which formed the monumental gateway to the Acropolis. With a central hall and two wings, it had five gates leading to the city above.

The western portico has six imposing double-columns (Doric on the outside and Ionic inside) and the ceiling was painted dark blue with gold stars. The northern wing was used as a picture gallery (with couches for officials) and the southern wing was the antechamber of the Temple of Athena Nike.

Top: Catch some Classical Greeks on display at the Acropolis Museum.
Above: Monument of Agrippa, still standing.

Neil Setchfield

It remained intact until the 13th century when a succession of occupiers began adding to it, including a Frankish tower later removed by Heinrich Schliemann.

One of the Propylaia's gates led to the **Panathenaic Way**, the route taken by the Panathenaic procession at the end of the festival dedicated to Athena, cutting through the middle of the Acropolis. It began at Keramikos and ended at the Erechtheion.

Statues once lined the path. The 8m-high pedestal on the left before the Propylaia once held a statue of a man riding a chariot, presumed to be a monument to victory at the Panathenaic Games. It is inscribed to a Roman benefactor, but archaeologists suggest it was reinscribed from a monument to an earlier victory.

The **Temple of Athena Nike**, built by Callicrates (c.420BC), is perched on the south-western edge. Only fragments remain of the frieze that ran around the temple, which depicted victory scenes from battles *(nikae)*. Some parts are in the Acropolis Museum. A statue of Athena once graced the temple, which was dismantled by the Turks and replaced by a canon. (The temple was dismantled in early 2002 and removed for restoration. It will be re-erected by 2004.)

The **Erechtheion** was built on the most sacred part of the Acropolis – where in a contest for the city, Poseidon struck the ground with his trident producing a spring of water and Athena in turn produced the olive tree (she won).

Named after Erichthonius, the mythical king of Athens, the temple was completed in 406BC and housed the cults of Athena, Pos-

Neil Setchfield

*Caryatid casts: one of their sisters is a castaway in the UK.*

eidon and Erichthonius. The six maidens that support the portico instead of columns are the famous Caryatids, modelled on the women from Karyai. The ones you see are plaster casts. The originals (except for one taken by Lord Elgin) are in the Acropolis Museum.

Apart from the workshops where archaeologists painstakingly restore and catalogue the site's fragments, the only other new building on the hill is the **Acropolis Museum**.

Don't leave without seeing this museum, as it contains many sculptures and reliefs from the site. The exhibits are in chronological order, from temples pre-dating the Parthenon, which help you imagine what a stunning sight it was.

## Moonlight

An exciting initiative has been the opening of key archaeological sites in Greece during the full moon in September.

Moonlight concerts in the Roman Agora, which proved a success in 2001, are expected to become an annual event. The Acropolis is magical to visit by moonlight and should not be missed.

Check the listings in the paper or on the website **e** www.culture.gr.

# THE PARTHENON (7, L4)

The symbol of the glory of ancient Greece, the Parthenon (Virgin's Chamber) stands on the highest point of the Acropolis. It is the largest

Neil Setchfield

## INFORMATION

- ✉ Acropolis
- ☎ 01 0321 0219
- e www.culture.gr
- Ⓜ Akropoli
- ⏱ May-Oct: 8am-6.30pm (winter: to 4.30pm)
- $ €5.87; under 18s & EU students free, other students & seniors half-price (inc museum & Acropolis)
- ⓘ Opens once a year for full moon, see p. 17

Doric temple ever completed in Greece and the only one built entirely of Pentelic marble (apart from its wooden roof).

As well as housing the great statue of Athena, the Parthenon served as the treasury for the Delian league. Built on the site of at least four earlier temples dedicated to the goddess (and patron of Rome) Athena, it was finished in time for the Great Panathenaic Festival of 438BC.

The temple had eight fluted Doric columns at either end and 17 on each side ingeniously curved to create an optical illusion of a harmonious, perfect form. Brightly coloured and gilded sculptured friezes that ran all the way around (159.5m long) depicted the various battles of the times and the Panathenaic procession. Most of the friezes were damaged in the 1687 explosion, but the greatest existing sections (more than 75m) are of the controversial marbles now in the British Museum in London.

The ceiling of the Parthenon was also painted blue and dotted with gold stars. The holy *cella* (inner room), reserved strictly for privileged initiates, contained the colossal 432BC statue of Athena Parthenos, covered entirely in gold and ivory, which was considered one of the great wonders of the ancient world. The tyrant Lachares is said to have stripped the gold from the 10m-high statue to pay his men. The cella is now only open to VIPs.

## Lost your Marbles?

The new Acropolis Museum, being built on the southern slope of the Acropolis, has been designed with a place intended for the Parthenon Marbles in the hope that international pressure will shame the British Museum into returning them before the museum opens in 2004.

The marbles were prised off the Parthenon in 1801 by the British Ambassador in Constantinople, Lord Elgin, who sold them to the museum, which in turn scrubbed them in the false belief that they should be white, when in fact they were colourfully painted.

**DON'T MISS**
- the 6th-century Kora (maiden) statues in room 4 of the museum
- superb views from the platform • Nike unfastening her sandal in room 8 • the *moschoforos* (calf-bearer) with his gift to Athena

# ANAFIOTIKA                                    (7, L5)

The neighbourhood located under the Acropolis, known as Anafiotika, is one of the most picturesque districts in the city, a labyrinth of quiet, narrow, windy streets where bougainvillea cascades over the houses and bright pots of colour decorate the balconies and rooftops. And, there are (almost) no cars.

The whitewashed Cycladic-style cube houses were built by tradesmen from the small island of Anafi who were brought in to build the king's palace during the rebuilding of Athens after Independence. It is still the home of many descendants of the Anafi stonemasons, although other artists and intellectuals have also moved in.

There are also many meticulously restored neoclassical houses, and derelict old homes that are crumbling. Washing hanging in the

*Back in 5 mins...*

## Ancient Foundations

Many of the Byzantine churches were built on the site of ancient temples in an attempt to crush the Pagan elements of the city – some have visible segments of temples used in the new structure.

Most of the churches still operate today, and the traditional Easter services attract people from all over Athens.

breeze is often the only evidence of habitation in the neighbourhood, apart from the forever-reclining cats.

The 17th-century church of **Agios Georgios** (St George of the Rock) marks the southern border of the Anafiotika, with the 1847 church of **Agios Simeon** situated to the north. The neoclassical building on the corner of Theorias and Klepsidra is the old university of Athens, now a museum.

*Pssst...hey, wanna buy some Byzantine art? Take a look at Thiamis on page 73.*

# ANCIENT AGORA                    (7, K2)

The best-preserved *agora* (market) in Greece gives invaluable insight into the workings of the ancient city. The **Agora** was the centre of civic life and a bustling hub of social activity.

It was the centre of government and housed the law courts and the market. This is where Socrates came to expound his philosophy and later, in AD49, St Paul came to win converts to Christianity.

**INFORMATION**

✉ Adrianou, Monastiraki (enter from Polygnotou)

☎ 01 0321 0185

ⓔ www.culture.gr

Ⓜ Monastiraki, Thissio

🕐 Tues-Sun 8.30am-3pm

⑤ €3.52/1.76

Neil Setchfield

First developed in the 6th century BC, it was destroyed by the Persians in 480BC, then rebuilt and flourished until AD267 when the Heruli, a Gothic tribe from Scandinavia, destroyed it. A residential area built on the site by the Turks was demolished after independence.

There is a useful model of this huge and confusing site in the **Agora Museum** in the **Stoa of Attalos**, which also has a collection of finds. The 45-column, two-storey stoa was essentially an expensive shopping arcade and hangout of rich Athenians, where they came to watch the Panathenaic procession.

It was authentically reconstructed in 1953-6 by the American School of Archaeology. More than 400 modern buildings were demolished to uncover the Agora.

The **Temple of Hephaestus**, the so-called 'Thisseion' on the western end, was dedicated to the god of the forge, and was surrounded by foundries and metal workshops. Built in 449BC, it is the best-preserved Doric temple in Greece, with 34 columns and a frieze on the eastern side depicting nine of the 12 labours of Heracles. Converted to a church in AD1300, the last service held there was in 1834, in honour of King Otto's arrival.

The site has many significant ruins and foundations from other buildings, including the **Stoas of Zeus Eleftherios** (Freedom), **Basileios** (Royalty) and **Poikile** (Painted Stoa), the **Metroon** (Record office), prison and the **Tholos** (where civic dinners were held).

## Supreme View

The massive Ancient Agora is best appreciated from above. The ideal bird's-eye view is from **Areopagus Hill,** which you reach from just below the Acropolis entrance.

Areopagus was the site of the supreme court where murder, treason and corruption trials were heard before the Council of the Areopagus.

This is where St Paul delivered his famous sermon in AD51 and gained his first convert, Dionysos, who became the patron saint of Athens.

**DON'T MISS**

● headless statue of Roman emperor Hadrian ● great drain & in situ inscribed boundary stone ('I am the boundary of the Agora') ● fine Byzantine frescoes in the 11th-century Church of the Holy Apostles

# BENAKI MUSEUM (6, E3)

Housed in the stunning former home of the Benaki family, this is the oldest private museum in Greece and ranks among its best. It was founded in 1930 by Antonis Benakis, son of the wealthy Alexandrian merchant Emmanuel Benakis, who was from a distinguished family of the Greek Diaspora.

The museum's collection represents the historical and cultural development of Greece and Hellenism. It includes his eclectic acquisitions from Asia and Europe and pieces from the Byzantine and post-Byzantine eras. It has also been the recipient of many significant collections and major donations since it was handed over to the state in 1931.

A 10-year, US$20 million renovation completed in 2000 refurbished all the galleries. There is a fine restaurant on the terrace overlooking the National Gardens and an impressive gift shop has been expanded.

More than 20,000 items are on display chronologically over four

**INFORMATION**

- ✉ Koumbari 1 (cnr Vas. Sofias), Kolonaki
- ☎ 01 0367 1000
- e www.benaki.gr
- Ⓜ Syntagma
- ⊙ Mon & Wed-Sat 9am-5pm (Thurs to midnight), Sun 9am-3pm
- ⑤ €6
- ♿ yes
- ✖ on-site restaurant

levels, beginning with prehistory to the formation of the modern Greek state. It has an excellent Byzantine collection and a gallery focusing on the development of Hellenism during foreign domination.

*Stony-faced exhibits at Benaki Museum*

The spectrum of Greek cultural history is covered, including Karaghiozi shadow puppets, a stunning array of costumes, jewellery, textiles, and paintings, including early works by El Greco.

The antiquities collection includes Bronze-Age finds from Mycenae and Thessaly and Cycladic pottery, while the Egyptian collection includes fayum Greco-Roman funerary portraits.

Benakis' heart is immured inside the museum's entrance, but the soul of Greece is well-enshrined in his gift to the country.

**DON'T MISS**

- Euboia treasure with 3000BC gold & silver cups ● Mycenaean gold jewellery from Thebes ● 2 signed El Greco paintings ● 2 mid-18th-century woodcarved reception rooms from Kozani mansions

# BYZANTINE & CHRISTIAN MUSEUM (6, E4)

Having undergone a major expansion and modernisation, the Byzantine and Christian Museum has become one of the city's pre-eminent galleries.

## INFORMATION

✉ Vasilissis Sofias 22, Athens

☎ 01 0723 2178

ⓔ www.culture.gr

Ⓜ Evangelismos

🕐 Tues-Sun 8.30am-3pm

⑤ €1.50; extra charge for special temporary exhibitions

ⓘ summer: Byzantine & classical music concerts held in the grounds.

♿ free entry (ground floor galleries only)

✗ on-site restaurant & cafe planned

BYZANTIUM

Neil Setchfield

A priceless collection of Byzantine and post-Byzantine art showcases the glory of Byzantium. Long overshadowed by ancient Greece, Byzantium is slowly claiming its rightful place as a significant epoch in history.

The museum has been housed in the elegant Tuscan-style villa of the French Duchess de Plaisance since 1930. That wing remains virtually unchanged, including the reconstructions of the three basic church types on the ground floor.

Only a fraction of the museum's collection of more than 15,000 artefacts from Greece and other reaches of the Byzantine empire is currently displayed.

Visitors can see icons from the 9th to 19th century, early Christian sculptures, wall paintings, frescoes, ceramics, exquisite embroideries, jewellery and a precious collection of ecclesiastical vestments and secular items in gold and metal, including the Mytiline treasure.

The new exhibition spaces – more than 4000 sq m – have gone underground and currently house temporary exhibitions, although a complete reorganisation of the museum's collection is expected by 2004.

Along with increased gallery space, there will be a restaurant and cafe and an amphitheatre for performances. The current gift shop has some exquisite icons.

*Home to countless Byzantine treasures*

DON'T MISS
• mosaic icon of the Virgin: *The Episkepsis* • 2-sided, 13th-century icon with St George on the front in gallery 7 • 4th-century sculpture of Orpheus playing the lyre surrounded by animals

# FILOPAPPOU HILL/HILL OF THE PNYX (7, L1)

Also known as the Hill of the Muses, pine-clad Filopappou is south-west of the Acropolis and has great views of the Acropolis and beyond to the plains of Attica and the Saronic Gulf.

The **Monument of Filoppapos** stands on the summit, built in AD114-16 in honour of prominent Roman governor, Julius Antiochus Filopappos. The tomb decorated by a frieze shows him driving his chariot.

A fort to defend Athens was built here in 294BC. It is a pleasant walk to the hill, starting from a paved path next to the Dionyssos taverna on Dionysiou Areopagitou.

On the way, you pass the 16th-century **Church of Agios Dimitrios Loumbardiaris**. According to a story dating back to the 17th century, a Turkish garrison on the Acropolis tried to fire a cannon on Christians gathered at the church on the saint's day, but the gunners were killed by a thunderbolt. Loumbardiaris is said to be a bastardisation of 'Bombardiaris' (bomber).

Sensitively restored in the 1950s, the church has some fine frescoes and is popular for baptisms and weddings. On the first day of Lent, 'Clean Monday', Filopappou is invaded by thousands of people picnicking and flying kites, as is customary throughout Athens.

North of Filipappou is the smaller **Hill of the Pnyx**, the meet-

**INFORMATION**

- ✉ off Dionysiou Areopagitou, Filopappou
- e www.culture.gr
- Ⓜ Akropoli
- ⑤ free
- ⓘ festival of Agia Marina is celebrated 17 July with a colourful street fair

*Breathtaking views from Filopappos Hill*

ing place of the Democratic Assembly in the 5th century BC. Aristides, Demosthenes, Pericles and Themistocles were among the great orators who addressed assemblies here. A chorum of 5000 was needed to vote.

North-west of the Pnyx is the **Hill of the Nymphs**, site of the old Athens Observatory.

Further down the hill is the **Church of Agia Marina,** which has a lively annual festival. Filopappou has many other smaller paths for walks and is popular with joggers, but caution should be exercised at night.

## Hill of Dance

Since 1965, Filipappou Hill has been the venue for lively performances of traditional Greek music and dance by the renowned **Dora Stratou Theatre** (see p. 95). The company has given more than 5000 performances before an audience of more than 2.6 million.

# KAISARIANI MONASTERY (1, D4)

The lush forest and gardens surrounding the 11th-century monastery of Kaisariani, nestled on the slopes of Mt Hymmetus, make this a wonderful sanctuary in the city.

Athenians come here for picnics and walks and despite being only 5km from town it's so peaceful; you cannot see or hear the sprawling city below.

## INFORMATION

- ✉ Mountain road starting at Ethnikis Antistaseos, Kaisariani
- ☎ 01 0723 6619
- 🚶 20min ride
- 🚌 take the 223 & 224 buses from Akadimias, but it's a 2km uphill walk from the bus terminus
- ⏱ Tues-Sun 8.30am-3pm (grounds open sunrise-sunset)
- 💲 €2.35
- ⓘ The ticket booth sells postcards & CDs of Byzantine music; church has 2 services a year: the Presentation of the Virgin on 21 Nov and the colourful Epitaph ceremony on Good Friday at 3pm
- ✗ bring a picnic

Neil Setchfield

Much of the pine forest was destroyed during WWII and the monastery itself had long crumbled into ruin. It was restored in the 1950s and reforested by the Athens Society of the Friends of the Trees.

The monastery was built on the foundations of an ancient temple and is dedicated to the Presentation of the Virgin. Four columns from the ancient temple support the dome of the church.

The walled complex has a central court around which are the kitchen and dining rooms (closed after being damaged in the 1999 earthquake), the monk's cells and the bath house.

The *katholikon* (main church) is built in cruciform style, highlighted with a dome. Most of the well-preserved frescoes on the walls and ceiling date back to the 17th and 18th centuries. The earliest frescoes, on the narthax, were painted in 1692 by Ioannis Hypatios from the Peloponnese. The adjacent chapel dedicated to Agios Antonios and the bell tower are later additions.

In its heyday in the late 12th and early 13th centuries, there were 300 monks and the monastery was a cultural centre. The monks were spiritual leaders, made thyme honey and wine and kept a rich library (destroyed by the Turks during the War of Independence). The monastery enjoyed considerable privileges and survived Frankish and Ottoman occupation.

Athenians once came here to drink from the 'magical' springs to aid fertility, but the water is low and undrinkable these days.

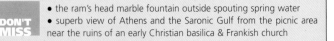

**DON'T MISS**
- the ram's head marble fountain outside spouting spring water
- superb view of Athens and the Saronic Gulf from the picnic area near the ruins of an early Christian basilica & Frankish church

# KERAMIKOS CEMETERY (7, H1)

As well as being the largest and best-preserved classical necropolis, the Keramikos cemetery is a little oasis in an otherwise noisy industrial corner of Athens.

It is also the site of the once-massive **Dipylon Gate**, where in antiquity the processions entered the city on their way to the Acropolis via the Ancient Agora. These days you have to search for the plaque that marks the ruins of the gate, but it all starts to make sense as you see the Acropolis ahead.

You can also see the site of the **Sacred Gate** through which pilgrims entered to travel along Sacred Way to Eleusis.

Named after the potter's workshops which once thrived in the area, the cemetery was the burial ground for Athenians from 3000BC to the 6th century AD. The grand Street of Tombs, where the elite Athenians were buried has some impressive tombs, notably the 4th century BC marble bull in the plot of Dionysos of Kollytos. The one in situ is a replica – the original and many other precious finds, including pottery, funerary offerings, toys and even knucklebones

**INFORMATION**

✉ Ermou 148, Thisio
☎ 01 0346 3552
e www.culture.gr
Ⓜ Thissio
🕐 Tues-Sun 8.30am-3pm
$ €1.47/88c

Neil Setchfield

Neil Setchfield

*Preserved forever, the tombs stand guard.*

sets, are in the Oberlaender Museum on the site.

Less visited than many other sites, it is green and peaceful and a delight in spring when the wildflowers are in bloom. Turtles crawl about, while frogs inhabit the spring that runs through the site.

Excavation work for an aborted metro station next to the site (it was diverted after major protests) uncovered a wealth of treasures, including more than 7000 *ostraka* (shards of pottery marked with the names of ostracised Athenian statesmen) that were buried there.

## Athens Archaeological Walk

Athens key archaeological sites are being linked in a massive €4.4 million project creating pedestrian paths and open space around the city. Already, the busy Dionysiou Areopagitou thoroughfare under the Acropolis has been transformed into a pleasant cobbled pedestrian precinct. The unification project will eventually link the ancient Panathenaic stadium with Plato's Academy to the west via the Temple of Olympian Zeus, Acropolis, Filopappou Hill, Ancient and Roman agoras and Keramikos cemetery.

# LYKAVITTOS HILL (7, G9)

If you are not game to walk, a funicular railway behind Kolonaki takes you through a tunnel to the peak of Lykavittos. The name means 'hill of wolves' but these days there is barely a dog on the rocky crag, which rises 272.7m.

Neil Setchfield

Floodlit at night and rising starkly from the sea of apartments below, Lykavittos is the other hill that dominates central Athens, along with the Acropolis. At night the view is spectacular and the air is cool, but even during the day this is a great place to get some perspective on the Athens panorama (pollution and summer haze permitting).

On a clear day you can see the island of Aegina and the Peloponnese from the top, and wonder why it takes so long to get to the beach when it is not that far at all. There are walking paths through the cypress and pine-covered hill.

On the peak the white **Chapel of Agios Georgios,** which is floodlit at night, stands on the site of an ancient temple that was once dedicated to Zeus. From the streets below it looks like a vision from a fairy tale.

There's an overpriced restaurant situated on the top of the hill monop- olising the superb views, and another cafe facing the other side. Further down, the shady Prasini Tenta cafe is a worthy alternative for lunch or a relaxing sunset drink.

## Open-Air Concerts

Each summer, the **Theatre of Ly- kavittos,** hosts rock concerts and the- atre in the evenings. The open-air amphitheatre (shown right) is one of the cooler literally) venues in town, with sensational views from the top rows. The surrounding rockface is often dotted with precariously perched people getting a free show.

Neil Setchfield

# MUSEUM OF CYCLADIC & ANCIENT GREEK ART (6, E4)

This exceptional private museum houses the biggest private collection of Cycladic art in the world. The museum was custom-built in 1986 for the personal collection of Nicholas and Dolly Goulandris, one of Greece's richest shipping families. It was expanded to include bequeaths and donations of Ancient Greek art and in 1992 took over the stunning 19th-century Stathatos mansion, designed by Ernst Ziller.

The two buildings are connected by a glass corridor. Temporary exhibitions are held in the Stathatos wing, including the recent long-running collection of major finds from excavations for the Athens metro.

The museum's collection is well displayed, lit and labelled and presented largely chronologically over three floors. Although it includes pieces right back to AD400, the emphasis is on Cycladic civilisation from 3000 to 2000BC.

The distinctive, minimalist slender figurines of the Cycladic era have long inspired modern artists and sculptors, including Picasso, Modigliani and Henry Moore.

The Cycladic collection, on the 1st floor, includes life-sized marble statues, tiny figurines and pottery from the civilisation that flourished in the Aegean during the Bronze Age.

Unlike other periods in history, Cycladic art, with its raw human forms, celebrates the individual rather than gods, deities and leaders.

The pleasant atrium cafe is a great pit-stop and the gift shop is well worth exploring.

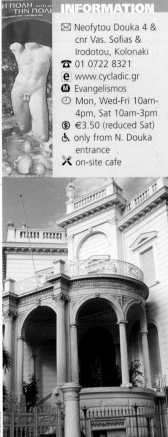

**INFORMATION**

✉ Neofytou Douka 4 & cnr Vas. Sofias & Irodotou, Kolonaki
☎ 01 0722 8321
ⓔ www.cycladic.gr
Ⓜ Evangelismos
🕐 Mon, Wed-Fri 10am-4pm, Sat 10am-3pm
⑤ €3.50 (reduced Sat)
♿ only from N. Douka entrance
✗ on-site cafe

Neil Setchfield

*Museum of Cycladic & Ancient Greek Art*

**DON'T MISS**

• Cycladic 'Modigliani' c.2800-2300BC (1st flr, case 1) • Drinker c. 2800-2300BC (1st flr, case 17) • 5th-century BC water jug (2nd flr, case 24) • Athenians at the Symposion (2nd flr, case 32)

# NATIONAL ARCHAEOLOGICAL MUSEUM (7, D6)

The bad news is that the museum housing the world's finest collection of Greek antiquities will be closing for major renovations. The good news is that the 1874 museum will be transformed into a modern facility, befitting the guardian of such a priceless collection. The dated museum, complete with some faded hand-written labels and guidebooks that have not changed for years, will be completely refurbished and upgraded in time for the 2004 Olympics.

**INFORMATION**

✉ Patission 44, Athens
☎ 01 0821 7717
e www.culture.gr
🚇 Viktoria
🕐 summer: Tues–Sun
   8.45am–6.45pm,
   Mon 12.30pm–
   6.45pm; winter:
   8.30am–3pm
💲 €6
♿ good (lower floors)

Neil Setchfield

Neil Setchfield

Top: Helmeted warrior c.490BC
Above: ancient Mycenean jewellery

The top floor of the museum has been closed since the 1999 earthquake, which sent many of its ancient pots tumbling.

Showpiece Minoan frescoes uncovered in Santorini have been returned to the island and many other galleries have closed. Half of the museum's collection languishes in storage due of lack of space. Its treasures do include, though,

antiquities from the Cycladic, Minoan, Mycenaean and Classical periods – sculpture, pottery, jewellery and countless other objects excavated throughout Greece.

There are many masterpieces, including a marble statue from Delos of Aphrodite with Pan and Eros c. 100BC, a life-sized Cycladic figurine from Amorgos (the largest ever found) and a bronze statue believed to be Poseidon or Zeus dating from 460BC. There is also an amusing sculpture of Aphrodite raising her sandal to ward off a frisky Pan (p. 13).

The museum is a must-see whatever state it might be in.

## Agamemnon's Death Mask

One of the most-visited exhibits is the exquisite Mycenaean gold collection from Grave Circle A at Mycenae, excavated by Heinrich Schliemann in 1847–76. The finds correspond with Homer's famous tale in the *Iliad* and *Odyssey*. Despite modern dating techniques suggesting it belonged to an earlier king, the 16th-century BC gold funerary mask (below) long believed to be Agamemnon's is a star attraction.

# NATIONAL GALLERY OF ART     (6, E6)

Greece's premiere art gallery celebrated its centenary in December 2000 with the opening of a refurbished wing to house its permanent collection of modern Greek art and sculpture. The €3.4 million facelift and extension added 2000sqm of exhibition space and installed the latest technology, including and advanced audio system with CD tours in English and Greek.

The history of Greek art is presented in chronological lines and themes exploring the country's unique art movements. Prize exhibits include three masterpieces from El Greco (Domenicos Theotokopoulos), including *The Burial of Christ*, acquired in 2000 for US$700,000, and *St Peter*.

The art exhibition begins with a small post-Byzantine collection,

**INFORMATION**

- ✉ Vasileos Konstantinou 50, Hilton
- ☎ 01 0723 5857
- e www.culture.gr
- Ⓜ Evangelismos
- ◷ Mon & Wed-Sat 9am-3pm, Sun 10am-2pm
- ⑤ €6.50
- ⚷ yes

Neil Setchfield

followed by the Eptanesian school artists originally from the Ionian islands, and who led the transition from Byzantine to secular painting. It then traces the years after Independence through to the work of renowned 1930s artists such as Yiannis Tsarouchis and Nikos Hadjikyriakos-Ghikas.

Postwar artists don't get as much wall space, but this is to be remedied in the second stage of the gallery's expansion – another 6,000 sq m of exhibition space is expected by 2004. The Alexandros Soutzos Sculpture Museum will be moved to a new gallery in Goudi.

The gallery also hosts major international exhibitions in the front wing, including the 1999 El Greco retrospective which attracted record crowds.

*Top: Abstract sculpture in front of Gallery*
*Above: Mural detail, National Gallery*

**DON'T MISS**

- Vrysakis' *Exodus from Messolongi* • Gyzis' *Behold the Celestial Bridegroom Cometh* • surrealist Engonopoulos' *Delos*
- Lytras' *The Kiss* • El Greco's *Concert of Angels*

# ROMAN ATHENS                                    (9, E3)

Under Roman rule, the city's civic centre was moved to the **Roman Agora**. The partly excavated site features the foundations of several structures, including a 1st-century, 68-seat public latrine to the right of the entry, and a *propylon* (entrance) on the south-eastern corner.

*Gate of Athena Archegetis (the Leader)*

The main surviving feature is the well-preserved **Gate of Athena Archegetis**, flanked by four Doric columns, which was erected in the 1st century AD and financed by Julius Caesar.

The octagonal **Tower of the Winds**, next to the Agora, is thought to have pre-dated the Agora, built about 150-125BC by the Syrian astronomer Andronicus. It is considered an ingenious construction, functioning as a sundial, weather vane, waterclock and compass. Made of Pentelic marble, it had a bronze triton as a weather vane and reliefs depicting the wind patterns.

The tower was converted to a church and then used for Dervishes under Ottoman rule. (The **Fethiye Djami** mosque on the northern side of the Agora is one of the few remaining reminders of Ottoman times.)

Near the Agora is the **Library of Hadrian**, once the most luxurious public building in the city. Erected in the 2nd century AD, it had an internal courtyard and water feature and was bordered by 100 columns.

Unfortunately, the site is closed to visitors but you can see the western facade, the ancient gateway and some of the niches of the library in the distance.

## Going Underground

Even if you don't plan to take a train, a visit to Syntagma's splendid metro station is a must. All gleaming marble and spotless, it is a veritable museum displaying finds uncovered during excavations.

Construction of Athens' underground rail network turned into Greece's biggest ever archaeological dig. Graves, foundations of ancient structures, ancient wells and thousands of artefacts were found in the process, causing major delays. Many of the finds are exhibited in the metro stations, with excellent displays at Akropoli and Evangelismos.

# SYNTAGMA                                    (7, J6)

The square at Syntagma is crowned by the grand **Parliament**, originally built as a palace for King Otto, the Bavarian prince installed by the allies after Greek Independence. It remained a royal palace until 1935, when it became the seat of the Greek Parliament. (The royals moved to the building that became the presidential palace when the monarchy was abolished in 1974.)

The Parliament is guarded by *evzones*, wearing the traditional uniform of short skirts and pom-pom shoes. On the hour, every hour three replacements march up Vasilissis Sofias and arrive for a colourful changing of the guard ceremony (every half hour the two guards swap ends). On Sundays and on major holidays, the evzones come out in the full regalia for an extended ceremony.

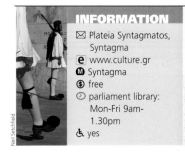

**INFORMATION**

- ✉ Plateia Syntagmatos, Syntagma
- 🅴 www.culture.gr
- Ⓜ Syntagma
- Ⓢ free
- ⊘ parliament library: Mon-Fri 9am-1.30pm
- ♿ yes

Neil Setchfield

Evzones groupies can go to the back of the Parliament gardens (on Irodou Attikou) and the presidential palace for more changing of the guard ceremonies.

Since the metro works finished, the square has regained some of its former grandeur and become a public meeting space. Each December it hosts Europe's largest Christmas tree.

The historic Grand Bretagne hotel was built in 1862 to accommodate visiting dignitaries, a role it maintains today. The Nazis made it their head-quarters during the war and it was the site of an attempt to blow up Winston Churchill on Christmas Eve 1944. The refurbishment of the grand St George hotel next door, will hopefully counterbalance the McDonald's and fast food joints that line the other side of the square.

*'vzones stand guard at Athens' Parliament.*

### Pom-Pom Parade

The Parliament building on Plateia Syntagma is guarded day and night by the much-photographed *evzones* (guards traditionally from the village of Evzoni in Macedonia). Their somewhat incongruous uniform of short kilts and pom-pom shoes is based on the attire worn by *klephts*, the mountain fighters who battled so ferociously in the War of Independence.

# TEMPLE OF OLYMPIAN ZEUS (7, M6)

The colossal Temple of Olympian Zeus is the largest in Greece and took more than 700 years to build. The 104 towering Corinthian columns stood 17m high with a base diameter of 1.7m. Fifteen remain today – one lies on the ground having fallen in a gale in 1852.

The foundations of a small Doric temple dedicated to the ancient cult of Olympian Zeus (dated 590-60BC) lie on the site. Peisistratos began building a temple twice its size in the 6th century, but it was abandoned for lack of funds.

**INFORMATION**

- ✉ Vas. Olgas, Athens
- ☎ 01 0922 6330
- ⓔ www.culture.gr
- Ⓜ Akropoli
- ⊘ Tues-Sun 8.30am-
  2.30pm
- ⑨ €1.47/88c

Neil Setchfield

Neil Setchfield

*Corinthian columns stand the test of time.*

A succession of leaders attempted to finish the temple, making adjustments to the original plans along the way, which explains inconsistencies in the temple. Hadrian finally took credit for finishing the task in AD131. The temple had a giant gold and ivory statue of Zeus. In 2001, the temple was the setting for a musical extravaganza by Vangelis, used to launch NASA 's Mars space probe.

**Hadrian's Arch** once linked a thoroughfare heading past **Lysikrates Monument** along the **Street of Tripods**, where tripod trophies were dedicated to Dionysos by winners of ancient drama contests. Made of Pentelic marble, it was erected in Hadrian's honour in AD132, after the consecration of the temple, for which it was a kind of architectural preface. It was also intended to mark the border of the ancient and Roman cities. The inscription on the north-western frieze reads 'This is Athens, the ancient city of Theseus'. The frieze on the other side says 'This is the city of Hadrian, and not of Theseus'. The city's best-preserved example of Roman public baths lies west of the Themistoklean city wall in front of Hadrian's Arch.

## Lysikrates Monument

The 335-4BC monument was erected by Lysikrates, a *choregos* (sponsor) of the drama contests, to display the bronze tripod trophies.

The circular building, with six Corinthian columns and a frieze showing scenes from Dionysos' life, is the only choregic monument preserved almost complete.

In 1669, it was incorporated into a Capucin monastery and used as a library, in which Lord Byron allegedly wrote part of *Childe Harold*.

# THE THEATRES (7, L3)

The **Theatre of Dionysos**, on the south-eastern slope of the Acropolis, was built on the site of the venue of the famous Dionysia Festival, during which there were contests, men clad in goatskins singing and dancing, and the masses feasting and partying.

The first theatre, built in the 6th century BC was made of timber. During the golden age, politicians sponsored productions of the dramas and comedies of Aeschylus, Sophocles, Euripides and Aristophanes. Reconstructed in stone and marble by Lycurgus between 342 and 326BC, the theatre had seating for more than 15,000 spectators, with 64 tiers of seats. Only about 20 survive. An altar to Dionysos once stood in the middle of the orchestra pit. The thrones on the lower levels were reserved for dignitaries and priests – the grand one in the centre

## INFORMATION

✉ Dionysiou Areopagitou, Makrigianni
☎ 01 0322 4625
🅴 www.culture.gr
Ⓜ Akropoli
🕐 8.30am-2.30pm
Ⓢ €1.50/88c
ⓘ For information & tickets for performances at Herodes Atticus Odeon contact Hellenic Festivals Office (see p. 95).

was for the priest of Dionysos. It is identifiable today from the lion's paws and satyrs and griffins carved on the back. You can also see the labels on the VIP thrones, which were made of Pentelic marble, as opposed to the limestone seating for the plebs.

The **Herodes Atticus Theatre** was built on the southern slopes of the Acropolis in AD161 by the wealthy Roman Herodes Atticus in memory of his wife Regilla. The semi-circular theatre had a cedar roof over parts of the stage and an imposing three-storey stage building of arches.

Excavated in the late 1850s, the theatre was restored and reopened in time for the 1955 Hellenic Festival. It remains Athens' premiere – and most inspiring – venue for summer performances of drama, music and dance. The theatre is only open to the public during shows.

*See grand shows at a grand old venue.*

**DON'T MISS**
- 2nd-century BC relief of Dionysos' exploits (backstage) • the Asclepion
- Stoa of Eumenes, once the promenade for theatre audiences

# sights & activities

Sightseeing in Athens involves lots of walking, mostly around the centre and historic areas of Plaka and Monastiraki where the majority of museums and major sights are concentrated.

Beyond the usual tourist route however, there are many interesting neighbourhoods, each with a unique character. Venturing away from the centre can be very rewarding and will certainly give you a better glimpse of the spectrum of modern Athenian life.

## Plaka & Monastiraki

Overrun by tourists in summer, the historic neighbourhoods under the Acropolis nonetheless retain their charm. Locals still come to Plaka's tavernas and cafes, making it a lively quarter year-round. While many of the traditional stores on the main streets have been replaced by souvenir and jewellery stores, you can still wander off the tourist strip and get a glimpse of the old neighbourhood. Monastiraki is less picturesque, but arguably more interesting to walk around, with its curious mix of stores, the flea market and quirky corners such as Plateia Avyssinia.

*Find an object at Monastiraki Flea Market.*

## Exarhia

Many people love the earthiness of Exarhia, posh Kolonaki's poor, but stubbornly bohemian, neighbour. It is still popular with students and left-wing intellectuals due to its historic association with radical politics and the student movements of the junta era (it's near the university). Exarhia is also home to many cheap tavernas, rebetika clubs and small live-music venues.

### Off the Beaten Track

If you want to get away from the tourist bustle, you can't go wrong with a drive up to the Kaisariani monastery. Closer to town, the ancient cemetery of Athens at Keramikos is one of the more green, peaceful and less-frequented archaeological sites. Alternatively, you could visit the gallery and museum at Eleftherias Park and have lunch or coffee at To Parko, a bar-restaurant overlooking the park.

## Gazi

The revival of this former semi-industrial area started with the innovative transformation of the historic gasworks into an impressive cultural centre. Gazi is slowly becoming a happening place, especially at night. Many derelict buildings have been restored and turned into hip restaurants and bars, and big warehouses turned into nightclubs – and the trend is spreading to nearby Rouf.

# Glyfada

Since the airport moved, Glyfada has lost some of its spark and the closure of some of the illegal seafront clubs combined with the construction of Olympic venues may reduce its appeal until the area's new face emerges. Glyfada was once a resort town, but now it is more a pleasant suburb to visit in summer when the beach, bars and activities make it very lively.

# Kifissia

Leafy Kifissia was once a cool northern retreat, where rich Athenians had their villas. It still is, although it is now more a classy upmarket suburb with its own elegant character and great bars, restaurants and shopping. The mansions and tree-lined streets and gardens are a far cry from the urban centre – another world only 12km north of Athens.

# Kolonaki

Historically an elite residential neighbourhood, Kolonaki is the most flashy part of central Athens. The boutiques, expensive restaurants and galleries are concentrated around and off the main square, where the outdoor cafes are constantly full. It certainly has a buzz, but it risks becoming a freak show

*Dozing off in the National Gardens*

of pretenders and designer fashion victims. Things get more dignified away from the square up towards Lykavittos Hill and around Dexameni.

# Psirri

Often described as the Soho of Athens, tourists are slowly discovering Psirri, behind its deceptively seedy, no-go area facade. Psirri's narrow streets are bustling at night with people heading to a string of restaurants and bars that have opened in this newly fashionable district. Renowned for its live music, particularly a tradition of merry late Sunday afternoons, Psirri is lively long after Plaka has shut down. Several hip galleries have opened in disused warehouses, but it retains an offbeat mix of old stores, bakeries and workshops.

# Piraeus

Beyond its function as the main port of Athens, Piraeus is a bustling, chaotic city in its own right. Most tourists go there to catch a ferry, and in truth there aren't many sights for tourists, although the Archaeological Museum is excellent. The main attractions are the social hub around Marina Zea and the picturesque harbours such as Mikrolimano, which is lined with restaurants and bars.

# MUSEUMS

### Centre of Folk Art & Tradition (7, L5)

The rooms in the neoclassical home of famous folklorist Angeliki Hatzimichalis have been set up to depict the traditional Greek way of life, including an old kitchen and its stove and utensils and ceramic plates from Skyros. The museum also has traditional costumes, embroideries, weaving machines, ceramic vases and family portraits.

⊠ Agelikis Hatzimichalis 6, Plaka
☎ 01 0324 3972
Ⓜ Akropoli; Syntagma
🕐 Tues-Fri 9am-1pm & 5-9pm, Sat & Sun 9am-1pm ⓢ free

### City of Athens Museum (7, H5)

A former palace where King Otto and his consort Amalia lived during the 1830s while the royal palace was being built, it contains some of the royal couple's furniture (including the throne), costumes and personal mementos. There are paintings by leading Greek artists such as Gyzis, and prints and models of Athens in the 19th century.

⊠ Paparigopoulou 5 & 7, Panepistimiou
☎ 01 0324 6164
🄴 www .athenscity museum.gr
Ⓜ Panepistimiou
🕐 Mon, Wed, Fri-Sun 9am-1.30pm
ⓢ €2.05/1.03

### Epigraphical Museum (7, D6)

Housing one of the most important collections of Greek inscriptions, this library of stones has huge stone slabs representing official records, lists of war dead, and tribute lists showing annual payments made to Athens by its allies. A major feature is the decree of the Athenian assembly ordering the evacuation of Athens before the Persian invasion in 480BC.

⊠ Tositsa 1, Exarhia
☎ 01 0821 7637
🄴 www.culture.gr
🚊 Victoria 🕐 Tues-Sun 8.30am-3pm
ⓢ free

### Frissiras Museum

(7, L6) This is a new museum of contemporary European painting in two recently renovated neoclassical mansions in Plaka. There are more than 3000 works of art, focusing mainly on the human figure, and a cafe. The historic building at No 7 was designed by an unknown student of Ernst Ziller.

⊠ Monis Asteriou Tsagari 3 & 7, Plaka
☎ 01 0323 4678
🄴 www.frissiras museum.com
Ⓜ Syntagma 🕐 Wed-Fri 11am-7pm, Sat & Sun 10am-3pm
ⓢ €5.87/2.93
♿ excellent

*Strike a chord at the Museum of Greek Instruments.*

Neil Setchfield

## Museum of Greek Costume (6, D2)

Run by the Lyceum Club of Greek Women, the museum has a comprehensive collection of regional costumes and accessories. Many were originally used in dance performances, until the costumes were preserved as museum pieces. They are well displayed, in thematic exhibitions.
✉ Dimokritou 7, Kolonaki ☎ 01 0362 9513 e icostumuseum.le@hellasnet.gr Ⓜ Syntagma ⏲ Sept-July: Mon, Wed & Fri 10am-1pm Ⓢ free

## Museum of Greek Folk Art (7, L6)

This state-owned museum founded in 1918 and housed in the old Mosque was moved to Plaka in 1973. It has examples of folk art from 1650 to the present, including embroidery, weaving, costumes, shadow-theatre puppets, silverwork and wood-and-stone carvings. The 2nd floor has a reconstructed traditional village house and a wonderful collection of wall murals by renowned primitive artist Theophilos Hatzimichail.
✉ Kydathineon 17, Plaka ☎ 01 0322 9031 e melt@melt.culture.gr Ⓜ Syntagma ⏲ Tues-Sun 8.30am-3pm Ⓢ €1.47/88c

## Museum of Greek Popular Instruments

(9, E4) An interesting museum with an extensive collection of instruments dating from the 18th century. Visitors can use the headphones to listen to instruments such as the

gaida (Greek goatskin bag-pipes). The 1842 mansion is also home to the Research Centre for Ethnomusicology and its extensive archives. Recitals of Greek traditional music are held in the garden.
✉ Diogenous 1-3, Plaka ☎ 01 0325 0198 e inval@atlas.uoa.gr 🚇 Monastiraki ⏲ Tues & Thurs-Sun 10am-2pm, Wed noon-6pm Ⓢ free

## Ilias Lalaounis Jewellery Museum

(7, M4) The talents of Greece's renowned jeweller are showcased in this private museum with more than 3000 pieces on display. Different sections feature works inspired by various periods in Greek history, videos explain the process of jewellery making and goldsmiths demonstrate ancient and modern techniques of their craft. Educational programs in English for groups or children are available.
✉ Kallisperi 12 (cnr Karyatidon), Makrigianni ☎ 01 0922 1044 e www.lalaounis-jewelrymuseum.gr Ⓜ Akropoli ⏲ Mon & Thurs-Sat 9am-4pm, Wed 9am-9pm, Sun 10am-4pm Ⓢ €2.93/1.76, free entry Wed 3-9pm & Sat 9-11am

## Jewish Museum

(7, K6) Housed in a renovated 19th-century mansion, the museum traces the history of the Jewish community in Greece from the 3rd century BC through an impressive collection of religious and historical artefacts, folk art and costumes. Nearly 90% of Jews living in Greece, most in Thessaloniki, were killed during the Holocaust.
✉ Nikis 39, Plaka ☎ 01 0322 5582 e www.jewishmuseum.gr Ⓜ Syntagma ⏲ Mon-Fri 9am-2.30pm, Sun 10am-2pm Ⓢ €2.93/1.47

## Kanellopoulos Museum (7, K4)

The 1884 mansion on the northern slope of the Acropolis houses the Kanellopoulos family's extensive private collection, donated to the state in 1976. It includes jewellery, clay-and-stone vases and figurines, weapons, Byzantine icons, bronzes and other antiquities dating back to the 3rd century BC. Some disruption (but no closure) is expected as the museum expands into the building next door.
✉ Theorias 12 (cnr Panos), Plaka ☎ 01 0321 2313 Ⓜ Monastiraki ⏲ Tues-Sun 8.30am-3pm Ⓢ €1.47/88c

---

## Museum Cost & Opening Hours

All state-run museums and archaeological sites are free on Sunday from November to the end of March and on 6 March, 18 April, 18 May, 5 June and the last weekend in September. Anyone under 18 gets in free year-round, as do card-carrying EU students and teachers, and journalists. Students with ISIC cards get a 50% discount. Most are closed on Mondays.

## Museum of 20th Century Design (1, B4)

Fans of 20th-century interior design will love this museum charting the evolution of modern furniture by leading names such as Le Corbusier, Dali, Gaudi and Frank Lloyd Wright, to name a few. If you're truly inspired, you can always purchase pieces from the museum's retail store.
✉ **Patmou 4-12 (Technal Plaza), Maroussi ☎ 01 0685 0611, 01 0689 1690** e **info@technalplaza.gr** 🚇 **Irini** ⏱ **Mon & Wed 9am-6pm, Tues, Thurs & Fri 9am-8pm, Sat 10am-3pm ⑤ free**

## Museum of Traditional Greek Ceramics (9, D2)

An annexe of the Museum of Greek Folk Art, on the square at Monastiraki, the museum features an extensive collection of folk pottery and hand-painted ceramics. It is housed in the 18th-century Mosque (Tzami) of Tzisdarakis, whose minaret has been removed.
✉ **Aeros 1, Monastiraki ☎ 01 0324 2066** 🚇 **Monastiraki** ⏱ **Mon & Wed-Sun 9am-2.30pm ⑤ €1.47**

## National Historical Museum (9, B8)

Greece's grand first Parliament is now a museum specialising in memorabilia from the War of Independence, including Byron's helmet and sword, weapons, costumes and Greek flags. There are also paintings, Byzantine and medieval exhibits, photographs and royal portraits, all exhibited chronologically, illustrating the evolution of Greece from the fall of Constantinople in 1453.
✉ **Stadiou 13, Kolokotroni Sq, Syntagma ☎ 01 0323 7617, 01 0322 2266** e **nhmuseum@tee.gr** 🚇 **Syntagma** ⏱ **Tues-Sun 9am-2pm** ⑤ **€2.93/58c, Sun free**

## Nautical Museum (5, E5)

Founded in 1949, the museum's nine rooms bring alive the nautical history of Greece, with models of ancient and modern ships, seascapes by some the Greece's greatest 19th- and 20th-century painters, guns, flags and maps.
✉ **Akti Themistokleous, Freatida Sq, Marina Zea ☎ 01 0451 6264** e **nme@internet.gr** 🚇 **Piraeus, then bus 904** ⏱ **Tues-Sat 9am-2pm ⑤ €1.47/88c** 🚽 **good**

## Philatellic Museum (7, M8)

Stamp collectors will love this small museum near the Panathinaic stadium featuring the history of philately in Greece. Exhibits range from old mailboxes and scales to the 1886 printing plates from the first stamp designed by the Hellenic Postal service, featuring the bust of Hermes – and naturally a huge stamp collection.
✉ **Fokianou 2 & Stadiou Sq, Mets ☎ 01 0751 9066** 🚇 **Syntagma** 🚽 **2,4,11** ⏱ **Mon-Fri 8am-2pm (Mon & Wed 5-8pm) ⑤ free**

## Piraeus Archaeological Museum (5, D5)

The refurbished museum has exceptional antiquities from Piraeus and other sites in Attica, the Saronic Gulf and the island of Kythera, including finds from a Minoan sanctuary on Kythera. A star attraction is a life-sized 520BC bronze statue of Apollo, the oldest known full-length bronze in Greece.
✉ **Harilaou Trikoupi 31, Zea Marina, Piraeus ☎ 01 0452 1598** 🚽 **040 from Syntagma** ⏱ **Tues-Sun 8.30am-3pm ⑤ €1.47/88c non-EU students, €1.17 seniors** 🚽 **good**

## Theatre Museum (7, G7)

A fine collection of memorabilia from great moments and great actors of Greek theatre, from costumes worn in ancient dramas to displays dedicated to opera diva Maria Callas, actress Melina Mercouri and renowned director Karolos Koun. There are also stage sets painted by leading Greek artists, and props, photographs and programs.
✉ **Akadimias 50, Panepistimiou ☎ 01 0362 9430** e **www .theatre-museum.gr** 🚇 **Panepistimiou** ⏱ **Mon-Fri 9am-1.45pm ⑤ free**

## War Museum (6, E4)

The junta-era museum honouring the armed forces has fighter planes in the forecourt which you can climb into. Inside, there is an invaluable historical collection of war memorabilia from the Mycenaean period to the present, including weapons, maps, armour and models of battles.
✉ **Rizari 2 (cnr Vasilissis Sofias), Athens ☎ 01 0729 0543-4, 01 0724 4464** 🚇 **Evangelismos** ⏱ **Tues-Sun 9am-2pm ⑤ free**

# NOTABLE BUILDINGS & MONUMENTS

### Athens Town Hall

(7, G4) The 1874 town hall was abandoned for modern premises in the early 1980s. When Dimitri Avramopoulos took office in 1995, he moved the mayor's office back to its historic home and undertook a major restoration of the facade and interior. The chambers have stunning frescoes by leading artists Fotis Kondoglou and George Gounaropoulos, as well as a valuable collection of art on display.

✉ Athinas 63 (opposite Plateia Kotzias), Athens ☎ 01 0331 2420-2 e www.cityof athens.gr Ⓜ Omonia ⏱ summer: 8.00am-1pm; winter: 8.30am-2pm ⑤ various

### Gennadius Library

(6, C5) In 1922, businessman turned diplomat John Gennadius handed over his personal library of books on Greece (comprising more than 27,000 volumes) to the American School of Classical Studies. The fine neoclassical library, purpose-built to house the collection, has a stunning reading room and a fine art and memorabilia collection.

✉ Souidias 61, Kolonaki ☎ 01 0721 0536 e www.ascsa .edu.gr/gennadius/genn .htm Ⓜ Evangelismos ⏱ Mon-Fri 9am-5pm, Sat 9am-2pm ⑤ free

## Building Boom

The grandiose neoclassical trilogy of buildings on Akadimias is part of the legacy of the Hansen brothers, Theophile and Christian, the Danish architects who joined the neoclassical building frenzy after Independence.

Flanked by the two giant columns on which Apollo and Athena stand, the **Athens Academy** is considered Theophile's most impressive work in Greece. Completed in 1885, it was paid for by the Austro-Greek Baron Sina. The exquisite frescoes in the entrance depict the myth of Prometheus.

The ostentatious buildings were built using white Pentelic marble and incorporate highly decorative friezes. The more modest Senate house of the **Athens University** in the middle was designed by Christian. Theophile's staircase of griffins leads to the 1902 **National Library,** which has a stunning reading room (7, G6; Panepistimiou 28-32; Panepistimiou; Mon-Fri 9am-2pm; the rest of the library has extended hrs Mon-Thurs 9am-8pm).

*Athena, Athens' patron, stands on an Ionic column at the Academy of Arts & Sciences.*

### Numismatic Museum

(7, H6) The former home of renowned archaeologist Heinrich Schliemann, who excavated Troy and Mycenae, is an exemplary neoclassical building that is now the Numismatic Museum. It is worth a visit even if you have no interest in coins, as it has some beautiful frescoes and mosaic floors.

✉ Panepistimiou 12, Syntagma ☎ 01 0364 3774 e protocol@nm .culture.gr Ⓜ Syntagma ⏱ Tues-Sun 8.30am-3pm ⑤ €3.52/1.76

### National Theatre

(7, F3) Designed by Ernst Ziller and completed in 1901, the decorative columned facade of the National Theatre was inspired in part by Hadrian's Library. It served as the Royal Theatre exclusively for the King's guests until 1908 when the public was allowed in.

✉ Agiou Konstantinou 22, Omonia ☎ 01 0522 3242 e www .n-t.gr Ⓜ Omonia

# BYZANTINE CHURCHES & MONASTERIES

### Athens Cathedral & Little Metropolis
(9, D6) The ornate 1862 cathedral dominates the square on Mitropoleos, and is the archi-episcopal Greek Orthodox church of Athens. Far more historically and architecturally significant is the small 12th-century church of **Panagia Gorgoepikoos** (Virgin swift to hear) next to the cathedral. Known as 'Little Metropolis', the cruciform-style church was built from marble, and used reliefs and pieces of ancient and early Christian monuments. Built on the ruins of an ancient temple, the church is dedicated to Agios Eleftherios.

✉ **Plateia Mitropoleos, Monastiraki**
☎ 01 0322 1308
🚇 **Monastiraki**
🕐 **7am-7pm, Sun Mass 6.30am**

## Paying your Respects

Always dress respectfully when entering a church. The custom is to light a beeswax candle for yourself and your loved ones, making a small offering in the boxes provided.

The silver *tamata* (votive offerings) around icons represent special prayers, thus the depictions of different parts of the body when someone is ill, or a baby for childless couples (or Volkswagen beetle as found in one souvenir shop).

Easter is the biggest Greek Orthodox celebration in Greece and a busy period for Plaka's historic churches.

Try to catch a night-time service in the week before Easter, particularly on Palm Sunday, Easter Thursday or Easter Saturday.

### Kapnikarea (9, C4)
Right in the middle of the pedestrian shopping strip of Ermou is the Byzantine church of Kapnikarea, dedicated to the Presentation of the Virgin Mary. Completed in the 13th century, the cruciform-style domed church was nearly destroyed to make way for progress. It now belongs to the Athens University, which undertook its restoration.

✉ **Kapnikareas & Ermou intersections, Monastiraki** ☎ 01 0322 4462 🚇 **Syntagma; Monastiraki**
🚇 **Monastiraki**
🕐 **Mon, Wed & Sat 8am-2pm, Tues, Thurs & Fri 8am-12.30pm & 5-7.30pm, Sun 8-11.30am**

### Agios Nicholas Rangavas (7, L4)
The 11th-century Byzantine church was part of the palace of the Rangava family, which included Michael I and emperor of Byzantium. The church bell was the first installed in Athens after liberation from

*Prayer candles create a warm glow at Athens Cathedral.*

Neil Setchfield

the Turks (who banned them) and was the first to ring in 1833 to announce the freedom of Athens. It now hangs inside the church and is rung every year on 25 March.
✉ Pritaniou 1 (top of Epimarchou)
☎ 01 0322 8193
Ⓜ Akropoli ⊘ 8am-noon & 5-8pm

### Panagia Grigoroussa, Taxiarhon & Fanouriou (9, E2)
Every Saturday afternoon, worshippers arrive at this Plaka landmark for a special service to get their *fanouropita* cake blessed before sharing it with passers-by. The cake is supposed to help you find something lost or someone you may be seeking. It tastes pretty good, too.
✉ cnr Taxiarhon & Epaminonda (near Andrianou), Monastiraki
🚇 Monastiraki
⊘ Apr-Oct: 5.45pm; Nov-Mar: 4.45pm

### Sotira Lykodimou
(9, F9) The largest medieval structure (and only octago-

*Lost something? Find your way to Panagia Grigoroussa.*

nal Byzantine church) in Athens, it has served as the Russian Orthodox Church of Athens since 1847. Built in 1031 as part of a Catholic monastery, it was restored by Tsar Alexander II in the 1850s, who added the belfry.
✉ Filellinon (near Kythathineon)
🚇 Monastiraki

### Church of the Holy Apostles of Solakis
(9, F1) One of the oldest churches in Athens, built c. AD1000, this Byzantine church dominates the site of the Ancient Agora. During Ottoman rule it underwent many changes but was restored in the 1950s and contains frescoes transferred from the demolished Agion Spyridon.
✉ Ancient Agora
🚇 Monastiraki

## Dafni Monastery
One of the most splendid Byzantine monuments in Greece, the 11th-century Dafni monastery (1, C2; Iera Odos, Haidari; ☎ 01 0581 1558) was damaged in the 1999 earthquake and was unlikely to reopen until late 2003 at the earliest.

It has some wonderfully preserved mosaics considered masterpieces of the era. The monastery's name derives from the laurels sacred to the god Apollo, whose sanctuary once occupied the site.

The earthquake was the last in a long history of blows for the monastery – it's been sacked by crusaders, desecrated by Turks, occupied by Gothic Cisternian monks, destroyed by anti-pagan edicts of emperors and later turned into a barracks and mental institution.

Neil Setchfield

# GALLERIES

Greek art is not just the domain of the ancients. Athens has an active contemporary arts scene and numerous galleries exhibiting local and international artists. Many new galleries have opened (or older ones relocated) in warehouses in the emerging arts precinct around Psirri and Omonia.

*Art for the modern age*

### Artio (7, H4)

An established gallery, which moved to an old industrial building in trendy Psirri in 1999, Artio exhibits work by leading contemporary Greek and international artists.

✉ Pallados 3, Psirri
☎ 01 0321 1602
🚇 Monastiraki
🕐 Tues-Fri noon-4pm & 6-9pm, Sat noon-4pm (closed June 30-Oct)
💲 free

### Athens Municipal Art Gallery (8, A9)

Housed in a neoclassical building on Koumoundourou Square, the Municipality's collection includes 2355 works of art, half of which were acquired during 1930-40. The collection represents the history of Greek art and includes engravings and works by the architect Ernst Ziller.

✉ Pireos 51, Eleftherias Sq, Athens

☎ 01 0324 3023
🚇 Thissio 🕐 Mon-Fri 9am-1pm & 5-9pm, Sun 9am-1pm 💲 free

### Athinais Gallery (8, A4)

The 'Art Hall' in this modern, multipurpose space in the recently restored old Athens silk factory exhibits contemporary Greek art from the private collection of Dimitris Pierides. It is also home to Greece's first museum of Cypriot antiquities.

✉ Kastorias 34-36, Votanikos, Gazi ☎ 01 0348 0000 e www.athinais.com.gr
🚇 Metaxourgio (10min walk) 🕐 Mon-Sun 9am-midnight; gift shop Mon-Sun 11am-3pm & 7pm-11pm
💲 free ⚬ good

### Bernier/Eliades Gallery (8, C8)

A leading Athens gallery, which showcases prominent Greek artists and brings exhibitions from an impressive range of international artists, from abstract American impressionist to British pop and performance team Gilbert and George.

✉ Eptahalkou 11, Thisio ☎ 01 0341 3935 e bernier_eliades@attglobal.net; www.art net.com/bernier-eliades .html 🚇 Thissio
🕐 Tues-Fri 10am-8pm, Sat noon-4pm 💲 free

### Deste Foundation, Centre for Contemporary Art (1, C4)

Founded by international contemporary-art collector Dakis Ioannou, Deste is a popular restaurant, art shop, bar and meeting place for the arts set. Designed by New York architect/designer Christian Hubert, the former paper

*Take home a piece Greek art, Skoufa Gallery (p. 67).*

warehouse holds serious exhibitions of Greek and international artists. Deste also promotes promising young artists through its annual prize for contemporary art.

✉ **Omirou 8, Neo Psihiko** ☎ **01 0672 9460** ℮ **www.deste.gr** Ⓜ **Ethniki Amina** then 🚌 **A6, A7, B6, B7 (Pharos stop)** ☾ **Mon-Fri 11am-midnight, Sat noon-4pm (closed middle 2 weeks of Aug)** ⑤ **free; guided tours Sat 1pm** ♿ **good**

### Gounaropoulos Museum (6, E10)

The former home and studio of one of Greece's revered modern painters is now a museum displaying his paintings and some of his personal effects. George Gounaropoulos (1889-1977), known as Gounaro, worked in Greece and Paris and his distinctive work has been inspired by French and German impressionists.

✉ **Gounaropoulou 6, Zografou** ☎ **01 0777 7601** 🚖 **taxi** ☾ **Mon-Fri 9am-1pm, also Tues, Wed & Thurs 5-7pm** ⑤ **free**

### Ileana Tounta Contemporary Art Centre (6, A6)

The bar-restaurant overlooking a lovely garden should not distract you from the art in this progressive art space near Lykavittos Hill. Renovation works were planned for 2002, during which the gallery was planning to exhibit a few doors down, before reopening anew.

✉ **Armatolon & Klefton 48, Ambelokipi**

*Home to some priceless pieces, Athens Municipal Gallery*

Neil Setchfield

☎ **01 0643 9466** ℮ **www.art-tounta.gr** Ⓜ **Ambelokipi** ☾ **Tues-Fri 10am-2pm & 6-9pm, Sat 11am-3pm; cafe Tues-Sat 10am-3am** ⑤ **free** ♿ **good**

### National Museum of Contemporary Art (7, P3)

Only one level of this museum is operating, staging exhibitions of Greek and foreign artists. Major reconstruction of the landmark factory will transform the upper levels into a major gallery space by 2004.

✉ **cnr Kaliriois & Frantzi, Fix** ☎ **01 0924 2111-2** ℮ **protocol@emst .culture.gr** Ⓜ **Syngrou Fix** ☾ **Tues-Wed & Fri-Sun 11am-7pm, Thurs noon-10pm** ⑤ **€2.93/ 1.47, free on Thurs after 5pm** ♿ **good**

### Pierides Museum of Contemporary Art (4, A1)

Dimitris Pierides founded this museum to house his collection of more than 1000 paintings, sculptures, engravings and ceramics, mostly by post-WWII artists from Greece and Cyprus. It also has a library of modern Greek art and funds special publications on Cypriot Archaeology and 20th-century Greek art.

✉ **Vasiliou Georgiou 29, Glyfada** ☎ **01 0898 1729, 01 0898 1167** ℮ **art-gallery@about .com** 🚖 **taxi** ☾ **Mon-Fri 9am-2pm (6-8.30pm for special exhibitions), Sat & Sun 10am-2pm** ⑤ **free**

### Rebecca Camhi Gallery (7, K6)

A visionary who led the art scene's move into the warehouses of gritty downtown Athens, Camhi continues to present eclectic exhibitions of contemporary art from leading artists.

✉ **Sofokleous 23, Omonia** ☎ **01 0321 0448** ℮ **www.rebeccacamhi .com** Ⓜ **Omonia** ☾ **Wed-Fri noon-8pm, Sat noon-5pm (closes Sat 3pm in summer) or by appointment** ⑤ **free**

# PARKS & PUBLIC PLACES

### Areos Park (7, B7)
The city's biggest park, just north of the Archaeological Museum, is a good place to escape the madness during the day. Among its wide tree-lined avenues is a long line of statues of War of Independence heroes.
✉ Alexandras Ave (cnr Patission), Pedion Areos Ⓜ Victoria
$ free ♿ good

### Eleftherias Park Arts Centre (6, C7)
The old army barracks used as a prison during the junta era have been converted into two galleries which are used for temporary art exhibitions. The pleasant park also houses the Venizelos Museum, dedicated to the great statesman.
✉ Vasilissis Sofias Ave (Eleftherias Park), Ambelokipi

*Technical wonders can be found at the Technopolis.*

☎ 01 0723 2603
Ⓜ Megaro Moussikis
🕐 Tues-Sat 9am-1pm & 5-9pm, Sun 9am-1pm
$ free

### Technopolis (8, C6)
One of the most exciting new spaces in Athens has been the redevelopment of the 1862 gas factory into a stunning industrial park and cultural centre. The old furnaces and other industrial features have been maintained, along with the different stone buildings that made this a self-contained community, with a carpenter's shop, smelter, garage, restaurant, barber shop and clinic. It hosts regular multimedia exhibitions.
✉ Pireos 100, Gazi
☎ 01 0346 0981, 01 0346 7322 🚇 Thissio
🕐 Mon-Fri 9am-9pm during exhibitions
$ free ♿ good

### National Gardens
(7, K7) The former royal gardens, designed by Queen Amalia around the palace that is now the Parliament, are a great green refuge during the summer. Winding paths lead to ornamental ponds with waterfowl and a botanical museum which has interesting drawings, paintings and photographs. The cafe near Irodou Attikou is a pleasant spot for a break. There are entrances to the gardens from Vas. Sofias and Amalias.
✉ Amalias, Syntagma (next to Parliament)

## Bronze Athens
The imposing statue of War of Independence hero Theodoris Kolokotroni (7, J6) was the first of Athens' 63 bronze monuments to be chosen for restoration as part of an ambitious, internationally funded program.

The massive 1904 statue of the general mounted on his horse shines again after conservators removed the effects of years of soot, acid rain – and bird poop (outside the National Historical Museum on Stadiou).

*Kolokotroni statue, now sans bird poop*

Neil Setchfield

☎ 01 0721 5019
Ⓜ Syntagma ☺ 7am-
sunset ⑤ free ♿ yes
✕ on-site cafe

**Omonia Square** (7, F4)
This once-grand square had
deteriorated into an ugly,
seedy, busy, humungous
roundabout for years clad in
scaffolding as construction
proceeded on the metro
below. A major beautification program has seen the
government-funded restoration of the facades of the
remaining neoclassical
buildings. Planned changes
to traffic conditions and the
redevelopment of the
square will restore some of
its grandeur.
🚋 Omonia ⑤ free

**Zappeio Gardens**
(7, L7) Next to the
National Gardens, the
Zappeio's formal gardens
surround the majestic
palace built in the 1870s by
the wealthy Greek-
Romanian benefactor
Konstantinos Zappas. It was
used as the headquarters of
the Olympic Committee
for the 1896 Olympics held
opposite at the Roman
Stadium. Unless there's a
function on, the guards will
let you in for a look at the
stunning courtyard. The gardens are not closed at night,
and in summer the historic
Aigli outdoor cinema, bistro
and Bedlam bar make this a
cool place to hang.
✉ Amalias, Syntagma
(next to Parliament)
Ⓜ Syntagma ⑤ free
♿ good

### Athens 1st National Cemetery

In a city with limited open space, the cemetery (7, P7; Anapafseos & Trivonianou,
near Kalimarmaron Stadium; ☎ 01 0922 1621, 01 0923 6118; May-Sept 7.30am-
8pm, Oct-Apr 8am-5pm) is a pleasant, if quirky, place to enjoy a stroll through the well-
tended gardens and resting place of many rich and famous Greeks and philhellenes.
The lavish tombstones and mausoleums include works of art by leading Greek sculptors of the 19th century, including *The Sleeping Maiden* by Halepas, on the tomb of a
young girl. The tale is that someone places a red rose in her hand everyday.

The mausoleum of archaeologist Heinrich Schliemann is decorated with scenes
from the Trojan War from reliefs he discovered during excavations. Other famous
residents include statesman Harilaos Trikoupis, benefactors Antonis Benaki,
Georgios Averof and Theodoros Syngros; and War of Independence heroes Sir
Richard Church, Kolokotronis, Makrigiannis and Androutsos. More recent and popular graves include those of actress Aliki Vougiouklaki, film star and politician
Melina Mercouri and former PASOK prime minister Andreas Papandreou.

*The Mother of the Occupation*, a bronze statue (near the entrance) of a starved
woman clutching a baby to her breast, is a moving memorial for the 40,000 citizens who died during WWII.

Neil Setchfield

# ATHENS FOR CHILDREN

### Children's Art Museum (7, K6)

Founded in 1994 to promote creative development and cultivate a love of art, the Children's Art Museum is one of the few of its kind in the world. There are exhibitions or work by budding young artists and workshops for children to let their creative juices flow.

⊠ Kodrou 9, Plaka
☎ 01 0331 2631, 01 0331 3734
e contact @childrens artmuseum.gr; www .childrensartmuseum.gr
Ⓜ Syntagma ⊘ Sept-Jul: Tues-Sat 10am-2pm, Sun 11am-2pm
Ⓢ €1.47, children free

### Children's Museum

(7, H7) More playschool than museum, this delightful and innovative interactive centre has a range of activities aimed at encouraging learning and imagination. Damaged during the 1999 earthquake, it has re-opened with new exhibits and programs, but kept its popular chocolate-making session. Most of the activities are suitable for non-Greek speakers.

⊠ Kydathineon 14,

### Ducking Around

If you just want some open space for children to run around in, the area around the duck pond in the National Gardens is an ideal spot.

There is also a rather dreary little zoo which these days has mostly farm animals.

*Hands up if you want to make chocolate!*

Plaka ☎ 01 0331 2995-6 e www.hcm.gr
Ⓜ Syntagma ⊘ Tues-Sat 10am-2pm, Sun 10am-6pm Ⓢ free

### Goulandris Natural History Museum

(3, B3) Founded in 1965 to promote the natural sciences and the protection of Greece's wildlife habitats and endangered species, this museum has exhibits of all sorts of animal and plant life, fossils and other displays. The modern GAIA Centre around the corner has interactive displays.

⊠ Levidou 13, Kifissia
☎ 01 0801 5870
e goul@gnhm.gr
🚇 Kifissia ⊘ Mon-Thurs 9am-2.30pm, Sat & Sun 9am-2.30pm
Ⓢ €2.93/1.17

### Pedomania Club

(8, D8) This amusement centre, located in a lovely two-storey neoclassical mansion, has every type of distraction imaginable.

Geared towards children aged three to ten, various activities include dancing, aerobics, painting, muppet shows, PlayStations, Internet and multimedia facilities.

⊠ Amfiktionos 18a, Thisio ☎ 01 0345 1506
e www.paedomania .freeservers.com
Ⓜ Thissio
⊘ Mon-Fri 8am-3pm & 5.30-10pm, Sat & Sun 10am-3pm; (closed 1-20 Aug)
Ⓢ Mon-Fri (4.40, Sat & Sun (5.87
♿ good
✗ on-site cafe

### Railway Museum

(7, A2) Though not strictly for children, the collection of old steam locomotives, mine-trains, wagons, royal carriages and old Athens trams at this museum is sure to appeal to kids at heart. Highlights include an 1899 steam locomotive and passenger car from the famous rack railway of

Diakofto-Kalavrita and the smoking car of the train of the sultan of Abdul Aziz.
**✉ Liossion 301 & Siokou 4, Sepolia ☎ 01 0524 6580 Ⓜ Sepolia ⏲ Mon-Fri 9am-1pm, Wed 5-8pm & Sun 9am-1pm $ free**

**Spathario Museum of Shadow Theatre**
**(1, B4)** This is an exhibition of the famous Karaghiozi and his colourful band of shadow-theatre puppets. Founded in 1965 by Eugene Spatharis, the collection dates back to 1947. There are also Greek and English books on shadow theatre.
**✉ cnr Vas. Sofias & Ralli (Kastalias Sq), Maroussi ☎ 01 0612 7245 🚆 Maroussi 🚌 A7, B7 ⏲ Mon-Fri & Sun 10.30am-1.30pm, also Mon & Wed 5.30-7.30pm; summer: Mon-Fri 10am-1pm $ free**

# QUIRKY ATHENS

**Hellenic Cosmos**
**(8, E3)** Take a virtual reality trip into ancient Greece at this high-tech interactive museum. Enter the Kivotos time machine – with floor-to-ceiling screens – and go back 2000 years to a 3D ancient Miletus. Part of the Foundation of the Hellenic World, the centre can provide English guides on request.
**✉ Pireos 254, Tavros ☎ 01 0483 5300 e info@ime.gr; www.fhw.gr/cosmos 🚆 Kalithea ⏲ Mon, Tues & Thurs 9am-6pm, Wed & Fri 9am-9pm, Sat 10am-3pm, Sun 10am-3pm $ prices vary according to programs offered ♿ excellent**

**Limni Vouliagmeni**
**(1, E4)** The source of the water at this lake has never been found, as some divers have lost their lives discovering. But the lake is popular with winter swimmers who enjoy the constant 22°C temperature of part-salt/part-spring water, which has therapeutic mineral qualities.

It's a wonderful setting, with its sheltered rock face, manicured lawns and old-style cafe-bar frequented by a regular crew of elderly citizens in their bathrobes and bathing caps. Its gradual slope makes it good for kids.
**✉ Limni Vouliagmeni ☎ 01 0896 2239, 01 0896 2237 🚌 A2 (or E2 express in summer) to Plateia Glyfada & then bus 114 ⏲ summer: 6.30am-8pm; winter: 7.30am-5pm $ €3.81 ✗ on-site cafe-bar**

**Ancient Shipsheds**
**(5, D6)** In the exposed basement of an ordinary Piraeus apartment block are the ruins of three slipways from an ancient shipshed in Piraeus. Zea was the main base for the Athenian fleet, which had more than 196 shipsheds (the ancients used to drag their ships in to shore). In a great example of preserving the past while getting on with life, the ruins can be seen next to the pylons holding up the apartment block. It is lit at night and visible from the street.
**✉ Sirangiou 1 (cnr Akti Moutsopoulou), Piraeus 🚌 20, Sirangiou stop $ free ♿ good**

## Dining like the Ancients

Athens is not big on theme restaurants but it was only a matter of time before someone turned to ancient Greece for inspiration – and gimmicks. That said, **Archaion Gefsis** (Ancient Tastes; 7, E2; Kodratou 22, Metaxourgio, ☎ 01 0523 9661, Mon-Sat 12.30pm-2am) claims to have researched the matter in order to provide authentic flavours and dishes that give new meaning to the term retro.

It has turned the clock back 2500 years before potatoes, rice, tomatoes and many other staples dominated the modern Greek diet. Roast meats and fish prevail on the menu, served with purees of peas or chickpeas and vegetables. The portions are huge.

The theme extends to the decor and service. Diners are seated at solid wooden tables, served by waiters in flowing red robes. There are no glasses (the ancients used earthenware cups), and spoons instead of forks. Bookings are essential.

# KEEPING FIT

There's a variety of activities in Athens to keep your fitness and fun going.

**Diving** is a highly restricted activity in Greece due to the potential for pilfering antiquities. Contact the Union of Greek Diving Centres (☎ 010 922 9532) for information.

If **jogging** is your thing, the easiest and most pleasant place to jog in Athens is around the National and Zappeio gardens where a maze of paths run through a rare green oasis. If you are game for a harder run, Lykavittos Hill has some wonderful paths and great views of Athens (and you can always cheat by taking the funicular railway up and running down the hill back into town through Kolonaki).

Unfortunately for **swimmers**, hotel pools are the only option in the city and the best one is at the Hilton, which will be closed for renovations until early 2003. Some hotel pools allow non-guests to use their facilities but they can be expensive. The best bet is to head to a public beach, although they get very crowded on the weekends.

Athens is not flush with public **tennis** courts and many, such as the Athens Tennis Club, are mostly reserved for members and are difficult to get into. Glyfada Golf Club has two modern outdoor tennis courts open to visitors (€8.80 per person per hr). Many of the GNTO/EOT beaches also have tennis facilities.

## BOWLING

**Bowling Centre Kifissia (3, B3)**
A little retro in design, this centre has tenpin bowling, as well as pool tables and a games parlour.
✉ Kolokotroni 1 (Shoppingland Retail Centre), Kifissia ☎ 01 0801 5844, 01 0808 4662 🚇 Kifissia ⏰ 9am-2am (inc holidays) ⑤ Mon-Fri €2.34/3.52 after 5pm, Sat €3.52, Sun €4.69 ♿ yes (lifts)

## DIVING & SNORKELLING

**Aegean Dive Centre (4, E5)** This accredited dive centre offers daily boat and shore dives, night dives, boat trips and snorkelling. There is also a special Discover Scuba course for kids (in a pool).

Most dives are around Varkiza, and 1-2 days notice is required.
✉ Zamanou 53, Glyfada ☎ 01 0894 5409 📧 dive@adc.gr;

www.adc.gr 🚕 taxi ⑤ snorkelling €15/25 shore/boat; diving €32-50 depending on type of dive (€15 for children)

*Have a ball at the Kifissia bowling centre.*

## GOLF

**Glyfada Golf Course**

(4, A3) This 18-hole public course, overlooking the Saronic Gulf, includes a recently refurbished restaurant and bar, club rooms and Pro-Shop. Call well in advance for weekend bookings as this is the only golf course in town.
✉ **Konstantinos Karamanlis (behind Ellinikon airport), Glyfada** ☎ **01 0894 6820, 01 0894 2338**
📧 **glyfgolf@compulink .gr; www.glyfadagolf .gr/clubnotes.html**
🚕 taxi ⏰ Tues-Sun 7.30am-sunset, Mon from 1pm 💲 green fees Mon-Fri €51.17, Sat-Sun €52.82; club/buggy hire €20.54/5.87; electric cart hire €26.41 (18 holes); lockers free ✖ restaurant & bar

## GYMS

**Universal Studios**

(6, A10) Part of a major chain, this modern gym has the latest facilities including weights, machines, aerobics, massage, solarium, spa, sauna and *hammam* (steam bath). It's one of the few places that accepts casual members.
✉ **Farandaton 4, Ambelokipi**
☎ **01 0771 5510**
Ⓜ Ambelokipi (10min walk) 🚌 13 (get off at Mesogeion intersection) ⏰ Tues-Sat 24hrs, Sun-midnight, Mon from 7am 💲 €10.27 (day pass)

## SWIMMING POOLS

**Athens Holiday Inn**

(6, E7) This medium-sized outdoor pool is the best option in this part of town given Hilton has closed for renovations, but the price for a casual visit is pretty steep.
✉ **Mihalakopoulou 50, Ilisia** ☎ **01 0727 8000**
📧 **www.hiathensgreece .com** Ⓜ **Megaro Moussikis**
⏰ May-Oct: 10am-6pm
💲 €20.54

**Park Hotel** (7, C6)

The rooftop pool here is too small for anyone who is a serious lap swimmer, however it does have great views of Areos Park and Athens. There is a also snack bar and beer corner.
✉ **Alexandras 10, Areos Park**
☎ **01 0883 2711**

📧 **www.park-hotel.gr**
🚇 Victoria
⏰ 10am-6pm
💲 €14.67
✖ snack bar

## TENNIS

**Agios Cosmas Athletic Club** (1, E3)

This state-run athletics club opposite the site of the old airport has tennis courts, track and field, basketball courts and even table tennis. The facilities were to be upgraded in the winter of 2001.
✉ **Poseidonos, Elliniko**
☎ **01 0981 5572**
🚌 A2 (Agios Cosmas stop) ⏰ 7am-7.30pm
💲 €2.93 per hr (inc racquet hire)

---

### Sun-kissed Beauties

Until 2001, most of the beaches close to Athens were run by the GNTO/EOT in set-ups designed in the '60s. Private operators were due to take over by the summer of 2002 and undertake major upgrades of all facilities. The beaches have change rooms and snack bars, and stay open late during heatwaves. The following are in order of distance from Athens.

**Alimo** has tennis courts, a giant water slide and beach bikes and canoes for hire (1, E3; ☎ 01 0982 9853; €2.35/1.17; 8am-9pm).

Shallow waters at **Voula** make it ideal for children, as does the playground and giant water slide (1, E3; ☎ 01 0895 3248; €2.35/1.17; 7am-8pm).

**Vouliagmeni** has great facilities, including the modern En Plo cafe whose decks sits right over the water (☎ 01 0896 0906-7; €2.35/1.17; 8am-9pm).

At **Varkiza**, the upscale facility is part of the Astir Palace resort, with water-ski centre, jet skis, tennis courts, restaurant and bungalows for afternoon siestas (2, C7; ☎ 01 0894 8251; Mon-Fri €8.80, Sat & Sun €10.27; 8am-8pm).

Bus A2 from Panepistimiou (in front of The Academy) stops at Alimo and Voula. To get to Vouliamgmeni and Varkiza, get off at Glyfada and transfer to bus 115. In summer there are express buses all the way to Varkiza.

# out & about

## WALKING TOURS
## City Walk

Begin at Parliament House ❶ about 10mins before the hour if you want to catch the changing of the guards. Cross over to the historic Grand Bretagne hotel ❷, turn right at Stadiou, following it until you come to the Old Parliament building, now the National Historical Museum ❸.

The recently restored Kolokotroni statue points down Omirou. Follow it until you come to Panepistimiou, one of Athens most impressive boulevards of grand buildings. Cross over to the St Denis Catholic Cathedral and the unusual 1847 Byzantine-style Eye Hospital ❹.

distance 3km duration 1.5hrs
▶ start Ⓜ Syntagma
● end Ⓜ Monastiraki

Apollo and Athena stand above the Athens Academy ❺ on towering columns. Next door is Athens University and the stunning National Library with its marble-columned entry and murals in the portico.

Continue up to busy Omonia Square ❻, which is getting a major facelift. Cross to the left and head down Athinas, towards the markets of Athens. Pass the restored 1874 Town Hall ❼ and Plateia Kotzia.

The smell of olives, cheese and spices hits you as you approach Athens market. Go past the colourful meat market ❽, an Athenian landmark. Turn left at Evripidou and right into Eolou, a pleasant pedestrian walk leading to the Tower of the Winds, below the Acropolis.

On the way you pass the churches of Agia Chrysospiliotissa ❾ and Agia Irini. Stop at cafe Aiolis ❿ for a break before hitting the shops on Ermou or continuing to Pandrosou St into the heart of Monastiraki.

# Lykavittos Hill & Kolonaki

Start at Parliament House ❶, turn right into Vasilissis Sofias continuing until the end of the gardens. Cross over to the Benaki Museum ❷ and keep going along Vas. Sofias until you get to the Stathatos mansion, now a wing of the Museum of Cycladic Art ❸.

Turn left into Loukianou, which takes you past the former home of Venizelos, now the residence of the British Ambassador ❹. This is the steepest part of the walk.

Take the steps to Kleomenous. If you have had enough climbing, turn right and head to the Teleferik (funicular railway) terminal ❺, which takes you to the peak in less than a minute (the more adventurous should keep going to the base of the hill and take the path up).

On a clear day, you get superb views of Athens, Aegina and the Peloponnese. Visit the Agios Georgos chapel ❻. Sadly, a plaque pointing out what you are seeing below is obscured by graffiti. Avoid the overpriced cafe and restaurant and take the path down, where you will find Prasini Tenta cafe ❼, which also has great views.

Follow the path back down to Kleomenos, turn right, pass the St George Lycabettus Hotel ❽, walk through Dexameni Square ❾ and the outdoor cinema to Iraklitou and turn left at Tsakalof, continuing through the boutiques until you hit Kolonaki Square. Join the throng having coffee, hit the shops or nearby museums.

**SIGHTS & HIGHLIGHTS**

Parliament House (p. 31)
Benaki Museum (p. 21)
Museum of Cycladic Art (p. 27)
Teleferik (funicular railway; p. 26)
Chapel of Agios Georgos (p. 26)
Lykavittos Hill (p. 26)
Dexameni Square (p. 35)
Kolonaki Square (p. 35)

Neil Setchfield

*Raising walking to a high art.*

**distance** 3.5km **duration** 2.5hrs
▶ **start** Ⓜ Syntagma
● **end** Ⓜ Evangelismos

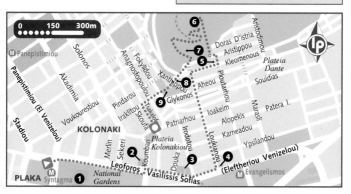

## Plaka & Monastiraki

From Parliament House ❶ cross over and walk through Syntagma Square ❷ (over Stadiou). Turn right at Mitropoleos and then left into Nikis.

You have now entered Plaka. The pedestrian area starts at Kydathineon. Stop at the Museum of Folk Art ❸, opposite the Church of Metamorphosis. At the square you can turn left at Geronta for a coffee at Tristrato ❹.

### SIGHTS & HIGHLIGHTS

Parliament House (p. 31)
Syntagma Square (p. 31)
Museum of Greek Folk Art (p. 37)
Tower of the Winds (p. 30)
Roman Agora (p. 30)
Ancient Agora (p. 20)
Stoa of Attalos (p. 20)
Library of Hadrian (p. 30)
Museum of Traditional Greek Ceramics (p. 38)
Monastiraki (p. 34)
Mitropoleos Cathedral (p. 40)
Church of Panagia Gorgoepikoos (p. 40)

Neil Setchfield

Back on Kydathineon, walk past the square and cafe strip and go right at Adrianou. Turn left at Flessa, where the pedestrian way ends, and veer right on Lyssiou until you get to the Tower of the Winds ❺ and the Roman Agora ❻.

Follow the Agora around and detour up Polygnotou to the Melina Mercouri Foundation where there are some interesting free displays.

From the Agora, turn left at Peikilis and right into Vrysakiou, which runs along the Ancient Agora ❼ and Stoa of Attalos ❽. Turn right into Adrianou and you end up not far from the Library of Hadrian ❾ and the Museum of Folk Art's Ceramics annexe ❿, and the square at Monastiraki ⓫.

Right into Pandrosou leads to Mitropoleos Cathedral ⓬ and the adjacent 12th-century Byzantine church, Panagia Gorgoepikoos ⓭.

Head back to Syntagma along Mitropoleos or detour left into parallel Ermou for some shopping.

**distance** 3km **duration** 2hrs
▶ **start** Ⓜ Syntagma
● **end** Ⓜ Syntagma

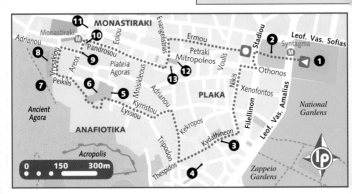

## Major Sights

From Parliament House, walk along the National Gardens ❶ at Amalias, turn left into the Zappeio Gardens and walk towards the Zappeion palace ❷. Stay on the path until you can see the old Olympic Stadium ❸ ahead.

Back across the road, walk along Vas. Olgas until you get to the statue of Byron ❹. Cross over to Hadrian's Arch ❺ and the imposing Temple of Olympian Zeus ❻.

Cross over Amalias and turn right into the pedestrianised walk on Dionysiou Areopagitou ❼. The Acropolis towers above as you head past the Theatre of Dionysos to the Herodes Atticus Theatre ❽.

Follow the theatre to the left until you get to the path heading up to the Acropolis ❾. Stop at the old Supreme Court foundations on Areopagus Hill ❿, and carefully climb up the slippery worn steps for a sensational view of Athens.

### SIGHTS & HIGHLIGHTS

Parliament House (p. 31)
Zappeio Gardens (p. 45)
Old Olympic Stadium (p. 9)
Temple of Olympian Zeus (p. 32)
Hadrian's Arch (p. 32)
Acropolis (p. 16)
Theatre of Dionysos & Herodes Atticus (p. 33)
Areopagus Hill lookout (p. 20)
Kanellopoulos Museum (p. 37)
Anafiotika (p. 19)
Church of Agios Georgios (p. 19)
Lysikrates Monument (p. 32)
Plaka (p. 34)

Keep walking along Theorias to the Kanellopoulos Museum ⓫. Continue along the base of the Acropolis until you get to the Agios Simeon Church ⓬. Walk around the back of the church, to the narrow streets of Anafiotika ⓭.

At the church of Agios Georgios ⓮, turn into the terraced park and walk out the gate down past Rangava St. To your left the path leads to the Church of Agios Nikolaos ⓯. Turn right into Tripodon and stop at the cute Amalthia cafe ⓰ or continue until you get to the Lysikrates Monument ⓱.

**distance** 4.5km **duration** 4hrs
▶ **start** Ⓜ Syntagma
● **end** Ⓜ Syntagma

Cross over to Adrianou, follow it up to Kydathineon and turn right towards the square ⓲ as you've no doubt earnt a rest at one of the cafes.

## EXCURSIONS
### Delphi      (2, A4)

## INFORMATION

*178km north-west of Athens*

- 🚌 Terminal B Liossion 260 (3hrs)
- ✉ Delphi
- ☎ 02 6508 2313 (museum)
- e www.culture.gr
- ⓘ Delphi tourist office (Vasileon Pavlos & Fredirikis; ☎ 02 6508 2900; Mon-Fri 7.30am-2.30pm)
- ⏲ summer: 7.30am-7pm; winter: 8.30am-3pm
- 💲 €3.52

*Doric columns at Delphi*

The ancient Greeks regarded Delphi as the centre of the world; according to mythology, Zeus released two eagles at opposite ends of the world and they met here at Delphi.

When you stand at the Sanctuary of Apollo in this spectacular setting, you can sense this is indeed a special place. Pilgrims once came here (around the 4th century BC) seeking the wisdom of Apollo's oracle. It was thought to literally be the mouthpiece of the god.

These days it's mostly tourists exploring the sanctuary and expansive archaeological sites. The refurbished museum has an excellent collection of finds from the site, including the celebrated life-sized bronze charioteer, whose piercing eyes follow you around the room.

If you come by car, visit the nearby village of Arachova or head down to the seaside village of Galaxidi for fresh fish at one of the seafront tavernas (about 30min drive).

*Amphitheatre where plays were held during the Pythian Festival (c.4th century BC)*

# Temple of Poseidon (2, D7)

The Temple of Poseidon is one of the most spectacular ancient sights in Greece, perched on the craggy cliffs of Cape Sounion, with the Aegean Sea making the perfect backdrop.

Sounion is best appreciated early in the morning or late afternoon when the tourist buses have gone and you can stick around for the stunning sunsets. In summer you can stop off along the coast for a swim.

Built in the 5th century BC on the site of previous sanctuaries, this is where the ancient Greeks worshipped the god of the sea. So inspired was Lord Byron when he visited in 1810 that he carved his name in one of the columns. Sixteen of the 36 Doric columns have been preserved.

Kim Wildman

*Marvellous marble Temple of Poseidon*

## INFORMATION

*70km south-east of Athens*
- 🚌 from Mavromateon (cnr Alexandras & Patission), Areos Park
- ☎ 0292 039 363
- ⓔ www.culture.gr
- ⏱ summer: 8am-sunset; winter: 10am-sunset
- ⓢ €2.35

# Nafplion (2, D5)

A popular weekend retreat, the beautiful seaside town of Nafplion is heritage protected. Its old quarter retains a wonderful mix of Greek, Venetian and Turkish architecture and the port is lined with stunning neo-classical buildings.

The imposing Palamidi Venetian fortress on the high cliffs above the town is an 800-step climb or a short taxi ride up, and it's worth it just for the view over the Gulf of Argos.

Briefly the capital of Greece during the War of Independence, Nafplion has been a major port since the Bronze Age. It is a charming place to visit, with many cafes, bars and restaurants along the pretty harbour, two other fortresses and plenty of sights to warrant a day trip.

## INFORMATION

*146km south-west of Athens*
- 🚌 Terminal A (Kifissou 100), departs on the hr
- ✉ Nafplion
- ☎ 07 5202 8036 (Palamidi fortress)
- ⓔ www.culture.gr
- ⓘ Nafplion's main tourist office (25 Martiou; ☎ 07 5202 4444; open 9am-1pm & 4pm-8pm) & the tourist police (☎ 07 5202 8131) are on the same street. May-June Palamidi hosts a folk music festival
- ⏱ summer: 8am-6.30pm; winter: 8am-4.30pm (Palamidi fortress)
- ⓢ €2.35 (Palamidi fortress)

## INFORMATION

*50km or 38 nautical miles from Piraeus*

✉ Hydra

☎ 02 0985 2205 (Hydra Tourist Police)

ℯ www.compulink.gr/hydranet

ⓘ Minoan Flying Dolphins run up to 9 hydrofoil services daily from Piraeus in summer & less frequently in winter (1.5hrs; €14.08 one-way); hydrofoil departure times: Piraeus Port Authority ☎ 01 0412 4585 or Minoan Flying Dolphins ☎ 01 0419 9000.

*Donkey backpacking around Greece.*

# Hydra                    (2, D6)

The island of Hydra, in the Saronic Gulf, is adored by artists and writers, and you can see why as soon as you enter the picturesque harbour. The gracious stone and whitewashed mansions line the surrounding hillside which is naturally shaped like an amphitheatre.

Adding to its charm is that fact that Hydra doesn't allow any cars or bikes (except for sanitation and construction vehicles) to drive on or around the island, so donkeys are the only means of transport.

Most of the action in Hydra is concentrated around the great waterfront cafes and shops, leaving the upper reaches virtually deserted. There is also a maze of winding streets to get pleasantly lost in.

The historic Lazaros Kountouriotis mansion on the hill has been turned into a wonderful museum under the auspices of the National Historical Museum.

## Ancient Olympia

The Olympic Games aren't quite returning to their birthplace in 2004. Ancient Olympia is 300km south-west of Athens (in the Peloponnese).

The first official quadrennial games were declared in 776BC in honour of Zeus, and took place on the first full moon of August.

The ancient site is in an idyllic lush setting and you can see ruins of a 2nd century BC gymnasium and wrestling school, among the other temples and structures. The museum has many important exhibits.

While it can be done by bus, it's a long trip and it may be best to join a tour (2, C3; ☎ 06 2402 3100; Mon-Fri 8am-7pm, Sat-Sun 8.30am-3pm; €3.52) or make it an overnight stay.

# ORGANISED TOURS

Most organised-tour companies offer a similar service and are normally booked through hotels or cater to package tourists. The day tours of Athens usually involve a drive-by tour of the sights stopping at one or two key sites, such as the Acropolis and its museum, so make sure you are clear on what you will actually get to visit. The sights are easy to get to on your own so, in many cases, the only real advantage is the guide. The night tours are pretty tacky and really aimed at tour groups. The best-regarded companies are Hop-In Sightseeing and Chat.

**Private Tours** The **Panhellenic Guides Federation** (9A Apollonos; ☎ 01 0322 9705; fax 01 0323 9200) can organise private tours by accredited guides to archaeological sites, with prior notice. Tour guide **Rania Vassiliadou** (☎ 01 0940 3932; **e** raniavassiliadou.virtualave.net), who has set up her own website, provides a well-regarded service around Athens' archaeological sites. Luxury yachting and adventure travel company **FYLY** (☎ 01 0985 8670; **e** www.fyly-extreme.gr) also organises custom-made special interest or VIP tours in and around Athens.

**Day Trips** Tours to **Delphi** include the archaeological site and museum and traditional village-cum-ski town, **Arachova**, famous for handmade carpets and quilts (Monday, Wednesday & Friday). The **Mycenae** tour includes stops at the **Corinth** canal, tomb of Agamemnon and other sights, lunch at Mycenae, a visit to **Nafplion** and the ancient theatre of **Epidauros** (Tuesday & Wednesday). Tours run 8am to 7pm and cost around €72.

## Wine Tours

Wine tourism has only been a relatively new phenomenon to Greece. The **Attica Wine Growers Association** (☎ 01 0922 3105 fax 01 0922 3115; **e** enoaa@ath.forthnet.gr) provides information and organises tours of local wineries participating in the Wine Roads of Attica program. The tours visit picturesque vineyards not far from Athens, as well as archaeological sites in the area. It is an ideal way to spend a day outside Athens.

**Island Tours** A day cruise (some with traditional dancing) to the islands of Hydra, Poros and Aegina can be fun and usually includes a buffet lunch and on-board tourist entertainment with traditional dancing. Chat's one-day cruise (7.45am-7.15pm; €66) stops at Hydra first, with time for a stroll or swim and sails to Aegina (via Poros but you barely have time to get off the boat), where for an extra charge you can take an excursion to the Temple of Aphaia. Hop-In does the same route in reverse, with lunch on board (8am-7pm; €66).

**Walking Tours** Free walking tours of the city's major archaeological sites, galleries and landmarks are held each weekend by **The City of Athens** (☎ 01 0323 1841; Sun & every 2nd Sat 10.30am). The tours are conducted in Greek but guides usually speak English and other languages. There are different destinations around town you can choose from.

### Hop In Sightseeing

Unlike other Hop On/Off tours, the **Hop In-Hop Out** tour follows a set route with stops at key sites, such as Parliament House, where people can get off, see the changing of the guard, check out the underground metro and hop back on. It drives past the main attractions but does not stop at every sight.

There is a 2hr stop at the National Archaeological Museum, followed by a tour of the Acropolis. The ticket is valid for 24hrs, so you can do a part of the tour the next day. Tours must be booked early on the morning of the same day or preferably the day before.

Departs 9am from Kallimarmaron Stadium, with pick-up points at Syntagma (8am) and Omonia (8.30am) and hotels.

✉ **Zanni 29, Pireaus**
☎ **01 0428 5500 (office open 6.30am-10pm)**
**e** **tours@hopin.com; www.hopin.com**
🕓 **Mon-Sun 8am-3pm**
⑤ **from €32.28/16.14 under 12**

### Fun Train

A cheat's way of seeing the sights, this little open-air mini-train weaves its way through the narrow streets of Plaka and the Thisio-Acropolis district. It's fun for big kids, too. The train departs from the Tower of the Winds near the Roman Agora, but it's best to call Hop In for directions and bookings.

🕓 **summer: daily 11am-7pm** ⑤ **€4.40 for 40min ride**

### Chat Tours

The **Athens Sightseeing** tour drives past the Tomb of the Unknown Soldier outside Parliament, the Olympic Stadium and several other key sites but the only stops are at the Temple of Olympian Zeus and the Acropolis, where you get a reasonable guided tour (9.15am-12.30pm; €41.90).

There are also half day afternoon tours (3pm-7pm; €28.80) that take you along the coastal road to **Cape Sounion** and the Temple of Poseidon.

✉ **Xenofontos 9, Syntagma**
☎ **01 0323 0827**
**e** **hermesgr@ ath.forthnet.gr**

### GO Tours

Catering to the big tour groups, this company has huge barn-like offices and provides a predictable set of short tours to the archaeological sites within Athens, as well as longer day trips.

✉ **Athanassiou Diakou 20, Makrigianni** ☎ **01 0921 9555** 🕓 **Mon-Sun 6am-9pm (office hrs)**

### Key Tours

Offers the usual selection of tours, the most popular and best organised being the half day Athens City Tour (€41.90) and the afternoon trip to Cape Sounion from 3pm-7pm (€27.87). The Athens-By-Night tour was a trip to a waterfront taverna in Piraeus – you are better off doing that alone.

✉ **Kalirois 4, Mets**
☎ **01 0923 3166**
🕓 **Mon-Sun 7am-8pm (office hrs)**

## A Bird's Eye View

You don't see choppers very often, but there are daily ½hr tours (including transport to/from hotel) from the old Ellinikon airport which fly over Piraeus and into city centre over the old Olympic stadium, around the Acropolis (you can't fly right over) towards Lykavittos, Kifissia and Ekali, then back to Ellinikon. The deluxe Eurocopter twin engine helicopters fly low (3000ft) for optimum viewing (runs daylight only; from €352.16 per person, min 2 passengers).

*Aerial view of Athens at dawn*

Juliet Coombe

# shopping

There are plenty of temptations for shopaholics in Athens, from wonderful handicrafts and exquisitely made shoes and jewellery, to cheap ancient motif souvenirs and tacky Acropolis lamps.

With high disposable incomes and an almost unhealthy consumer zeal, the brand-conscious Greeks shop with a passion, leading to a strong presence of big-name brands. New stores are constantly opening in a market that has become far more sophisticated in the past decade.

The most concentrated shopping strip is on Ermou, from Syntagma to Monastiraki, which must have more shoes per square metre than any other place in the world.

Most of the top boutiques are scattered around the nearby Kolonaki, while all the elite designers and jewellers, including

*Colourful jewellery from Kolonaki*

Louis Vuitton, Pentheroudakis and Bulgari, are on Voukourestiou, off Akadimias. Kifissia and Glyfada also offer great shopping.

Plaka and Monastiraki are full of souvenir and tourist stores that open until late. You can fit in a full day of museums and sites (or business) and still have time to buy souvenirs or spoil yourself with a unique piece of Greek jewellery.

The following guide is by no means definitive but suggests a range of stores to cover most needs – and a few stand-out favourites.

Be warned, some sales assistants can be a little in your face, greeting you immediately with a terse *'parakalo',* (a 'can I help you?' equivalent with a 'what do you want?' tone) and following you around the store. That said, most are friendly, speak English and are happy to assist.

During sale times (July to August and January to February), especially in July, there are some great bargains. Haggling is acceptable (and effective) in smaller, owner-run stores, particularly souvenir and jewellery shops (especially if you pay cash), but don't bother in major chains or department stores.

## Shop till you Drop

Trading hours in Athens are still influenced by the old days when people went home for lunch and a siesta during the heat of the day. The family-run shops reopened in the evenings, which is still the best time in summer to shop. But times are changing and many stores and businesses are now open all day, especially in the busy centre.

Official trading hours are: Tuesday, Thursday and Friday 9am-2pm and 5.30-8.30pm (winter: 5-8pm); Monday, Wednesday and Saturday 9am-3pm. In Piraeus, stores open 30mins earlier. Department stores are open Monday to Friday 8am-8pm, Saturday 9am-3pm.

These hours do not apply to tourist shops, which are usually open on Sunday and until late on weekdays.

# MARKETS

### Athens Central Food Market (7, G4)

The hectic, colourful Athens *agora* (market) is the highlight of the Athinas market strip. A visual and gastronomic delight with the most amazing range of olives, spices, cheese and deli treats leads you to the meat market, which can look quite surreal, with hanging carcasses illuminated by endless rows of swinging light globes.

The fresh fruit and vegetable market is nearby and there are some gems in the surrounding streets, including many old-style tavernas (see Diporto, p. 82). Catch some Greek blues and traditional music at the Stoa Athanaton (see p. 96) rebetika club that operates day and night.

✉ **Athinas (btw Sofokleous & Evripidou), Omonia** Ⓜ **Omonia** ⊙ **Mon-Sat 7am-3pm**

### Monastiraki Flea Market (9, C2)

Athens' famous flea market takes place Sunday, when traders spill out around Plateia Avyssinias and along Adrianou to Thisio. It isn't what it used to be, but it still has a distinctly festive atmosphere and is a must-see for visitors. The nearby cafes and restaurants are brimming – and there are certainly some bargains, interesting collectables and kitsch delights to be found among the junk. The permanent antique and collectables stores have plenty to sift through and

## To Market, to Market...

Almost every neighbourhood in Athens has its weekly designated street market known as the *laiki*, where you get the cheapest and best variety of fresh fruit and vegetables and an array of consumer goods.

The city's biggest market (Lagoumitzi, near Syngrou Ave, Neos Kosmos; Ⓜ Neos Kosmos; Sat 7am-2.30pm) is held just behind the Athanaeum Inter-Continental, on either side of the Lagoumitzi street overpass (and even on it).

The streets on the southern side, near the St Analipsis Church, are lined with stalls selling everything from manchester, underwear, tool and glassware to old cameras and bric-a-brac.

Cross the overpass for fruit and vegetables, fresh fish and an assortment of kitchenware, herbs etc. If you take the metro, follow the stalls and crowd down Kasomouli St.

the maritime theme runs strong. Many of these stores are open all week. This is the place to test your haggling skills.

✉ **Around Ifestou & Pandrosou, Monastiraki** 🚇 **Monastiraki** ⊙ **Sun 7am-3pm**

### Piraeus Flea Market (5, A5)

It was a blistering 40°C day when we visited, but you still had to fight the throng to get through this busy Sunday market. The makeshift stalls are set up along the streets around the railway

station, selling an assortment of stuff you find in markets everywhere – cheap clothing, shoes, tools, blankets and more junk than you could ever need. If it's antiques and collectables you're looking for, it might be better to venture out during the week when the area's antique shops are easier to get to.
**✉ centred around Alipedou, Great Harbour, Piraeus**
**Piraeus ⌚ Sun 7am-2pm**

Neil Setchfield
*This Athens-in-Wonderland tea set is among the weird and wonderful at the Monastiraki Flea Market.*

## DEPARTMENT STORES

**Fokas** (9, D8)
This five-storey department store resides in a restored neoclassical building in the hub of Ermou. It stocks a select range of men's, women's and children's wear labels, as well as travel goods, accessories, swimwear, beauty products, toys and books. In summer, a cafe operates on the outdoor terrace on the top floor.
**✉ Ermou 11 (cnr Voulis), Syntagma**
**☎ 01 0325 7740**
**Ⓜ Syntagma**

**Hondos Centre** (7, F4)
This 10-level super-store has just about everything, from designer clothes to sunscreen, an extensive range of swimwear, cosmetics and perfumes. It's particularly worth a visit during the sales. The rooftop cafe has great views of Athens and the Acropolis.
**✉ Omonia Square 4,**
**☎ 01 0522 1335, 01 0528 2800**
**Ⓜ Omonia**

**Lambropoulos** (7, F4)
More than 400 shops within the one big shop, Lambropoulos is one of Athens' oldest department stores, with Greek and imported labels in clothing and footwear, cosmetics, aesthetics and household goods.
**✉ Eolou 2-8 (cnr Lykourgou), Omonia**
**☎ 01 0324 5811**
**Ⓜ Omonia**

**Marks & Spencer** (9, D6) This reliable UK chain has a number of stores in Athens if you're looking for those familiar basics, especially underwear and more conservative clothing. It also stocks food and wine staples that you might not find elsewhere.
**✉ Ermou 33, Syntagma ☎ 01 0323 8459 Ⓜ Syntagma**

Neil Setchfield
*Those in the know flock to Fokas for some fine shopping on Ermou.*

# CLOTHING

## GREEK DESIGNERS

**Bettina (6, D3)**
The pond in the entrance with the faux waterlilies leads to three more under-stated levels of top-name fashion for all ages. Bettina stocks creations by London-based up-and-comer Sophia Kokosalaki, Angelos Frentzos and other well-known Greek and international designers.
✉ **Pindarou 40 (cnr Anagnostopoulou), Kolonaki** ☎ **01 0323 8759** Ⓜ Syntagma
🕐 **closed 15 Aug-25 Sep**

**Christos Veloudakis (6, D3)** A dramatic-looking boutique, the long red velvet curtains and racks of clothing are equally designed for maximum impact. This is women's and men's day-and-night wear with an edge.
✉ **Tsakalof 22a, Kolonaki** ☎ **01 0364 1764** Ⓜ Syntagma

**Elina Lebessi (6, D3)**
Elina has a great range of elegant and fun dresses and evening wear in fabulous fabrics, colours and original designs, with

*The latest in lingerie*

Neil Setchfield

matching handbags and accessories. Also stocks French designer Mia Oeser.
✉ **Iraklitou 13, Kolonaki** ☎ **01 0363 1731** Ⓜ Evangelismos; Syntagma

**Yiorgos Eleftheriades (6, D3)** One of Greece's cutting-edge designers, trained in costume design, Eleftheriades has developed a steady local clientele and is set to move into the European market. Alternative classicist, high design, hand-finished clothes for men and women, using natural fabrics.
✉ **Pindarou 38, Kolonaki**
☎ **01 0361 5278**
Ⓜ Evangelismos

## OVERSEAS DESIGNERS

**Carouzos (6, D4)**
A huge range of quality, stylish designs by leading men's and women's labels include Lanvin, Versace, Ferre, Fendi, Zegna and DKNY. It also stocks a selection of Prada bags and other big-name accessories.
✉ **Patriarhou Ioakim 14, Kolonaki** ☎ **01 0724 5873, 01 0724 5606**
Ⓜ Evangelismos

**Emporio Prince Oliver (6, D3)**
A major fashion importer, Emporio has its own product line as well as top international labels such as Paul Smith, Mathew Williamson, Helmut Lang, Paco Rabanne, Paul & Joe, Anna Sui and Yohji Yamamoto. **Prince Oliver 'Business'** (6, D2; Akadimias 18) has exclusive menswear and the latest in suits.
✉ **Anagnostopoulou 9, Kolonaki** ☎ **01 0362 7284** Ⓜ Syntagma
🕐 **Tues, Thurs & Fri 9.30am-3pm & 5-9pm, Mon, Wed & Sat 9am-4pm**

**Lakis Gavalas (6, D3)**
A popular choice for the fashion elite, this boutique is in Athens' most elite shopping neighbourhood, with the latest from Dior, Moschino, Exte, Earl Jeans and D&G.
✉ **Voukourestiou 50 (cnr Tsakalof), Kolonaki**
☎ **01 0362 9782**
Ⓜ Evangelismos; Syntagma 🕐 **Tues, Thurs & Fri 9am-3pm & 5-8.30pm, Mon, Wed & Sat 9am-3.30pm**

---

## Breaking the Fashion Barrier
The fashion-conscious Greeks have always had a strong local market, but the current generation of young designers is starting to make an impact on the international scene.

Leading designers such as Sophia Kokosalaki, Celia Kritharioti and Angelos Frentzos are cutting it on the catwalks and in the fashion houses of Europe and beyond. Other names to look out for include Markellos Nihtas, Yiorgos Eleftheriades, Ioannis Guia, Deux Hommes and Vasso Consola.

### Sotris (6, D3)

Sotris has three levels showcasing the latest fashion everything, from clothing to accessories by D&G, Miu Miu, Prada, Venetta Bottega and Greek-success story, Angelos Frentzos. You'll also find select home accessories, CDs, art and magazines.
✉ **Voukourestiou 41 (cnr Tsakalof), Kolonaki**
☎ **01 0361 0662**
Ⓜ **Syntagma**

### Vardas (7, G5)

Vardas sells men's and women's international designer wear and classic sportswear from Lanvin, Trussardi, Ted Lapidus, as well as made-to-measure suits.
✉ **Stadiou 44, Omonia**
☎ **010 3218600**
Ⓜ **Panepistimiou; Omonia**

## MAINSTREAM FASHION

### Acrobat (6, D3)

Affordable versions of the latest look for hip young things, Acrobat has its own clothing label, as well as brands such as Miss Sixty and Fornarina.
✉ **Skoufa 29, Kolonaki**
☎ **01 0821 2526**
Ⓜ **Evangelismos**

### Aerakis (6, D3)

Indulge here in the best French and Italian lingerie in feminine laces and silks of all colours and designs, swimwear, sleepwear, hosiery and bath products. The men's range is two doors up and carries the latest from Calvin Klein and Cotton Club.
✉ **Skoufa 1 (cnr Filikis Eterias), Kolonaki**
☎ **01 0362 4165**
Ⓜ **Syntagma**

> ## Tailor-made Perfection
>
> **Christakis** (6, D2; Kriezotou 5, Syntagma; ☎ 01 0361 3030) was a bit of an Athens institution, making shirts for politicians, royalty, diplomats and anyone who was anyone. His name and tradition continues at this exclusive tailor shop, which has rolls and rolls of wonderful shirt fabrics, in every possible shade of blue, as well as ready-made shirts and imported designer brands.
>
> Staff can usually turn out a shirt within the week (even sooner if it's urgent). But expect to pay for such luxury service – shirts starts at about €120.

### Artisti Italiani (9, D7)

Quality and fashionable takes on classic looks, as well as trendy designs in men's and women's clothing, for day and evening. Look out for the sales.
✉ **Ermou 22, Syntagma** ☎ **01 0331 3857** Ⓜ **Syntagma**

### Glou (9, C5)

Glou sells smart, affordable menswear, including casual and business suits and shirts, as well as mainstream sportswear and accessories.
✉ **Ermou 49, Syntagma** ☎ **01 0322 7575** Ⓜ **Syntagma**

### Oxford Company

(6, D4) A popular chain with an extensive selection of quality goods, Oxford has well-priced men's shirts, ties and other apparel for all occasions.
✉ **Patriarhou Ioakeim 12, Kolonaki**
☎ **01 0721 1133**
Ⓜ **Evangelismos; Syntagma**

### Zara International

(9, C5) This Spanish export brand has the most affordable fashion in Athens, thus the common chaotic scenes, especially on Saturdays (go early and on weekdays). A huge range of women's clothing and menswear, accessories, and children's wear.
✉ **Ermou 47, Syntagma** ☎ **01 0324 9930** Ⓜ **Syntagma**

*Rugged up mannequins at Artisti Italiani in Ermou*

# JEWELLERY & ACCESSORIES

**Accessorize** (9, C5)
This well-known UK chain has Athens' most extensive collection of beaded costume jewellery, great bags, swimwear and accessories. A fun and affordable way of adding colour and flair to your wardrobe. There's also a store at the airport.
✉ Ermou 42, Syntagma ☎ 01 0331 7780 Ⓜ Syntagma

**Archipelagos** (7, L5)
Unique pieces of silver and gold jewellery, trinkets and ceramics are sold here at very affordable prices. Look out for the fine silver bookmarks with tassles.
✉ Andrianou 142 (cnr Thespidos), Plaka
☎ 01 0323 1321
🚇 Monastiraki
🕐 daily 10am-9pm (later in summer)

**Byzantino** (7, K5)
Reputedly one of the best of the myriad stores in Plaka selling gold in ancient Greek motifs, the jewellery here is hand-crafted by the owners, which means the prices are very competitive.
✉ Adrianou 120
☎ 01 0324 6605
🚇 Monastiraki

**Demetriadis Art Wear** (6, D2)
A delectable selection of high-fashion bags, including exclusive designer ranges from Gaultier, Lollypop and XX1, as well as designer jewellery and their own bijoux.
**Solonos 15, Kolonaki**
☎ 01 0322 7329
Ⓜ Syntagma
🕐 Mon, Wed & Sat 10am-3.30pm, Tues & Thurs 10am-8.30pm

**Elena Votsi** (6, D3)
Votsi's refreshingly original work has been appreciated for years on the island of Hydra and now sells in New York and London. Her stylish new Athens store offsets her bold designs, which use gold, silver and exquisite stones to create works of art.
✉ Xanthou 7, Kolonaki
☎ 01 0360 0936
Ⓜ Evangelismos; Syntagma

**Fanourakis** (6, D4)
Delicate pieces of folded gold characterise Fanourakis' bows, insects and other unique creations. The distinctive designs are sheer art, a fact that is also reflected in the prices.
✉ Patriarhou Ioakeim 23, Kolonaki (also at Panagitsas 6, Kifissia)
☎ 01 0721 1762
Ⓜ Syntagma

**Folie-Follie** (9, C6)
A Greek success story, which has gone global since it started in 1986, you're bound to bump into one of these stores around Athens. There's a wide range of Bijoux jewellery,

## Jewels in Athena's Gown

Gold is not actually produced in Greece – all of it is currently imported. But the quality of workmanship gleaned from a 3000-year-old tradition – and the competition that comes from having thousands of gold and silversmiths – makes handcrafted Greek jewellery a great buy.

The past 50 years has seen a revival of interest in traditional designs and techniques for making exquisite gold and silver jewellery. More recently artists have turned to the craft, making modern jewellery one of Greece's most thriving and creative industries.

The big names in Greek jewellery, Lalaounis & Zolotas, have helped promote Greek jewellery worldwide. Lalaounis is the only jeweller to have been recognised by the French Academy of Fine Arts and his impressive jewellery museum, with a permanent collection of over 3000 designs, is worth a visit (see p. 37).

shawls, silk and leather bags and other colourful accessories.
✉ Ermou 37, Syntagma ☎ 01 0323 0601 Ⓜ Syntagma

**Ilias Lalaounis** (6, D1)
Lalaounis' exquisitely crafted, original creations are considered works of art, displaying new takes on ancient Greek motifs and inspiration from other cultures, biology, nature and mythology. Lalaounis jewellery is sold in top jewellery houses around the world.
✉ Panepistimiou 6 (cnr Voukourestiou), Kolonaki ☎ 01 0361 1371 Ⓜ Syntagma

**Mad Hat** (6, D3)
This small milliner's store is brimming with colour and character, offering hats of every style and finish, from casual straw beach hats to imaginative felt creations. There are also belts, handbags and other accessories.
✉ Skoufa 23, Kolonaki ☎ 01 0338 7343 Ⓜ Syntagma

**Metalo** (9, E8)
This tiny store carries its own designs in silver and gold, using semi-precious stones and pearls to create interesting, affordable jewellery. There are lovely worry beads and other delectable pieces.
✉ Mitropoleos 11, Syntagma ☎ 01 0322 7579 Ⓜ Syntagma

**Pentheroudakis** (6, D2)
This established and exclusive Athens jewellery house exhibits a select range of modern and simple, timeless pieces in

*Rings to make Liberace drool, Byzantino.*

precious metals and gemstones. There's also an exclusive array of high-end decorative gifts.
✉ Voukourestiou 19 (cnr Valaoriti), Kolonaki ☎ 01 0361 3187 Ⓜ Syntagma

**Petai Petai** (6, D3)
Small individual cabinets lining the walls contain a wonderful, eclectic collection of original designs, from casual silver pieces to handcrafted gold with precious stones. Owner Ioanna Kokoloupoulou presents her own creations, as well as pieces produced by leading designers, including the Leontaraki jewellery house, Erato Boukogianni, sculptor Vangelis Polizos and Vali Kontidou.
✉ Skoufa 30, Kolonaki ☎ 01 0362 4315 Ⓜ Syntagma

**Studio Eleven** (6, D2)
Silver and semi-precious stones entwined with colourful threads and delicate wires are some of the

simple, fun pieces made in this workshop.
✉ Kanari 17, Kolonaki ☎ 01 0362 6191 Ⓜ Syntagma

**Topaz** (9, E4)
This corner shop in the heart of Plaka has silver handmade jewellery, including the jeweller's signature range of tiny Cycladic houses and churches made into key chains, business card holders, earrings and brooches.
✉ Adrianou 67 (cnr Mnisikleous), Plaka ☎ 01 0321 4320 🚇 Monastiraki

**Zolotas** (9, B9)
Internationally renowned jeweller Zolotas breathes life into ancient Greece with replicas of museum pieces. Since 1972, the company has had the exclusive rights to make exact copies of the real thing.
✉ Stadiou 9, Syntagma ☎ 01 0331 3320 Ⓜ Syntagma

# SHOES & LEATHER GOODS

**Bournazos** (9, D7)
These Greek designs for men and women have gained international recognition for their quality, workmanship and style. Also stocks a good range of bags and leather accessories.
✉ **Ermou 15, Syntagma** ☎ **01 0325 5580** Ⓜ **Syntagma**

**Charalas** (9, C6)
A popular and affordable option on Ermou, Charalas has a wide selection of quality leather shoes and bags, from out-there latest fashion looks to the classics by Nine West.
✉ **Ermou 30, Syntagma** ☎ **01 0325 8100** Ⓜ **Syntagma**

**Danos** (6, D3)
Artful window displays showcase Danos' feminine, individual designs, made in Greece from the finest imported leathers. It also has a select range of international designs.
✉ **Filikis Eterias Sq 6, Kolonaki** ☎ **01 0362 5390** Ⓜ **Evangelismos**

**Fifty/Fifty** (9, C4)
You might find a real bargain here among the small selection of last season's sample half-priced bags by top brands such as Prada, Furla, Guess and Thiros. Look upstairs for more stock.
✉ **Ermou 57, Monastiraki** ☎ **01 0324 7128** Ⓜ **Monastiraki**

**Fontana** (7, G5)
Housed in a grand old arcade, Fontana carries a fantastic range of Italian, French and Greek leather diaries, wallets, briefcases, accessories and travel goods.
✉ **Arsakiou Arcade 3, Panepistimiou** ☎ **01 0323 2093** Ⓜ **Panepistimiou**

**Furla** (6, D3)
Classy, fashionable bags and accessories by this leading Italian label are well priced in Greece compared to New York or London.
✉ **Patriarhou Ioakeim 8, Kolonaki** ☎ **01 0721 6154** Ⓜ **Evangelismos**

**Kalogirou** (6, D3)
Shoe fetishists will love the range of designer offerings in colours and styles to blow the imagination and budget. It stocks top international names, as well as Kologirou's own creations. Avoid Saturday mornings or you will have to fight your way through the boutique set.
✉ **Patriarhou Ioakeim 4, Kolonaki** ☎ **01 0722 8804** Ⓜ **Evangelismos**

**Prasini** (6, D3)
Imelda Marcos would have gone nuts in this shoe heaven, with French, Italian, Spanish and Greek designer footwear for the really well-heeled, indeed. Not to mention the bags.
✉ **Tsakalof 7-9, Kolonaki** ☎ **01 0364 1590** Ⓜ **Evangelismos**

**Spiliopoulos** (9, C4)
It is usually chaotic, but there are bargains among the overcrowded racks of imported shoes and bags from top brands such as La Spiga, Kate Spade, Samsonite and Genny, usually at wholesale prices. It also stocks leather jackets.
✉ **Ermou 63, Syntagma** ☎ **01 0322 7590** Ⓜ **Syntagma**

**Thiros** (6, D2)
An established Greek label for well-priced leather bags of all shapes, in classic and contemporary designs. Everything from tiny purses to work and weekend bags.
✉ **Pindarou 21 (cnr Skoufa), Kolonaki** ☎ **01 0362 8445** Ⓜ **Syntagma**

*Purrr... fashionable fur at the Furla store*

Neil Setchfield

# ART & ANTIQUES

### Antiqua (9, E10)
Serious Greek and European antiques from the 15th-19th centuries are sold here, with a good selection of silverware, clocks, paintings and icons. Expect to pay accordingly.
✉ Amalias 2-4, Syntagma ☎ 01 0323 2220 Ⓜ Syntagma

### Antiquarius (6, D3)
A well-established specialist in imported antiques and collectables, mostly from the UK and France, items include books, prints, silver, crystal, embroideries and small furniture pieces.
✉ Anagnostopoulou 8, Kolonaki ☎ 01 0360 6454 Ⓜ Syntagma

### Athena Gallerie (9, E4)
This two-level gallery in Plaka has a large range of paintings, silkscreen prints and lithographs by leading Greek artists, as well as an exhibition space featuring guest artists.
✉ Mnisikleous 7b, Plaka ☎ 01 0331 5209 🚊 Monastiraki
🕐 Mon-Sat 10am-8pm (summer: 1-9pm), Sun 9am-5pm

### Dexippos Art Gallery
(9, E2) Most of the pieces here are commissioned from a group of skilled artists producing museum copies and original designs influenced by ancient Greece. Unique sculptures, frescoes, paintings and ceramics are bought by locals and discerning tourists.
✉ Dexippou 1 (cnr Panos), Plaka
☎ 01 0324 7688
🚊 Monastiraki

### Martinos (9, D3)
This Plaka landmark opened in 1926 and still has a great selection of Greek and European antiques, including painted dowry chests, icons, coins, glassware, porcelain and furniture.
✉ Pandrosou 50, Monastiraki ☎ 01 0321 2414, 01 0321 3110 🚊 Monastiraki

### Michael Mihalakos
(6, D2) A good place to hunt for collectables such as china, prints, paintings, glassware, silver, fancy light fittings and bigger furniture items.
✉ Solonos 32, Kolonaki ☎ 01 0362 6182 Ⓜ Syntagma
🕐 Tues, Thurs & Fri 8.30am-8.30pm, Mon, Wed & Sat 10am-3pm

### Moraitis (7, L5)
Takis Moraitis lives and works in his studio, where you will find his trademark landscapes from the Ionian islands and Cyclades. A great space with huge fireplace where you can occasionally see the celebrated artist and his students at work.
✉ Adrianou 129, Plaka
☎ 01 0322 5208
🚊 Monastiraki
🕐 daily 11am-11pm

### Paleopolion o Alexandros (8, C10)
This landmark store on Thisiou is bursting with collectables, crockery, amber worry beads, postcards and memorabilia such as commemorative plates featuring Greek royalty.
✉ Thisiou 10, Monastiraki ☎ 01 0321 2414 🚊 Thissio

*Antiquarius, Kolonaki*

### Skoufa Gallery (6, D3)
As well as regular exhibitions from local artists, the gallery has sculptures, paintings, prints and a select collection of small antique pieces and objets d'art.
✉ Skoufa 4, Kolonaki
☎ 01 0360 3541
Ⓜ Evangelismos

### Stavros Mihalarias
(6, D4) The art and antiques here are strictly for hard-core collectors, but the restored Kolonaki stately mansion is worth wandering through. Mihalarias is a world-renowned expert in the restoration of icons and fine art and holds art auctions annually.
✉ cnr Alopekis & Irodotou, Kolonaki
☎ 01 0721 0689
Ⓜ Evangelismos

### Zoumboulakis Gallery (6, D1)
This gallery has a fantastic range of limited edition prints and posters by leading Greek artists, including Tsarouhis, Mytara and Fassianos. Athens' best known contemporary art dealers also sell antiques from the Kolonaki store (Haritos 26), which caters to the top-end collector.
✉ Kriezotou 7, Syntagma ☎ 01 0363 4454 Ⓜ Syntagma

# CRAFTS, GIFTS & SOUVENIRS

### Aidini (9, F8)

You can see the craftsman at work in his little workshop at the back of the store. Well-priced original creations include small mirrors, candlesticks, boats and planes made from bronze, copper and other metals.

✉ Nikis 32, Plaka
☎ 01 0323 4591
Ⓜ Syntagma

*Olive wood – guaranteed to outlast the best of them.*

### Benaki Museum Gift Shop (6, E3)

Some of the best replicas of Greek artefacts, jewellery, prints and books are sold here, as well as an exquisite collection of icons, from reasonably priced copies to pieces worth a small fortune.

✉ Koumbari 1, Kolonaki ☎ 01 0362 7367 Ⓜ Evangelismos

### Centre of Hellenic Tradition (9, D3)

Upstairs in this arcade are great examples of traditional sculptures, woodcarvings, paintings and folk art from prominent Greek artists, plus antiques. The cute cafe/ouzeri has Acropolis views, and there's also a gallery.

✉ Pandrosou 36 (or Mitropoleos 59), Monastiraki

☎ 01 0321 3023
▣ Monastiraki
⏱ Mon-Sun 9am-8pm (winter: closes 1hr earlier)

### Dimitris Vasiliou (8, C10)

This newcomer to Athens sells ceramics featuring sea motifs, small mosaic mirrors and interesting jewellery from the artists on the island of Paros.

✉ Adrianou 1, Thisio
☎ 01 0331 6433
▣ Thissio ⏱ Tues-Sun 10am-2pm & 4-10pm

### Double Axe (9, D8)

This tiny store is easy to miss, but it's been around since 1925 and stocks beautiful handwoven tablecloths and rugs from Crete and other parts of Greece.

You'll also find ceramics, old and modern jewellery and all sorts of interesting knick-knacks.

✉ Voulis 23, Syntagma
☎ 01 0322 3783
Ⓜ Syntagma

### Eommex (9, E8)

A huge showroom run by a traditional cooperative selling folk art and designer rugs made by more than 30 weavers around the country. Displays change regularly.

✉ Mitropoleos 9, Syntagma ☎ 01 0323 0408 Ⓜ Syntagma

### Georgiadis (7, G4)

Located in the busy Central Food Market strip, Georgiadis sells classic tin kitchen accessories, from brightly coloured retsina/wine

## Fancy a Flokati?

There are endless possibilities for souvenirs, from small items such as worry beads, traditional fishermen's hats, charms and Greek sea sponges to high-end museum copies of ancient Greek art.

Plaka and Monastiraki are lined with stores selling *tavli* (backgammon) sets, colourful hand-blown glass, hanging oil lamps, Byzantine icons, hand-painted ceramics, handicrafts such as olive-wood key rings (pictured), *flokatis* (woollen rugs) and handwoven rugs. There is also a huge selection of handcrafted silver and gold jewellery, art and modern sculpture in ceramic, bronze and marble.

decanters, stainless steel olive oil pourers, aluminium trays, lanterns and even intricate wire mouse traps.
✉ **Sofokleous 35, Omonia** ☎ **01 0321 2193** Ⓜ **Omonia**
🕐 **Mon-Sat 7am-3pm**

### Keramar (1, B4)

A huge selection of pottery and ceramics from 170 workshops all over Greece, including hand-painted traditional ceramics, jugs and pots. It's a bit of a hike but it's a good place to go if you want pottery of any kind or one of those giant Cretan urns to ship home.
✉ **Kifissias 207, Maroussi** ☎ **01 0802 5332** 🚌 **550 (get off at Ageioplastiki stop)**
🕐 **daily 9am-9pm**

### Kori (9, E8)

One of the stand-outs among the squillions of tourist gift shops in Plaka, Kori has some lovely statues and figurines, ceramics, artwork and an eclectic selection of handcrafted jewellery.
✉ **Mitropoleos 13 (cnr Voulis), Plaka** ☎ **01 0323 3534** Ⓜ **Syntagma**

### Koukos (9, F7)

This is a wonderful collection of Italian pewter picture frames, platters, jugs, replicas of old monk's hip flasks and other items. Koukos also stocks a range of antique ceramics and original silver handcrafted jewellery.
✉ **Navarhou Nikodimou 21, Plaka**
☎ **01 0322 2740**
Ⓜ **Syntagma**

### Mati (9, B10)

Beautifully designed *mati* (blue-glass and silver

amulets to protect you against the evil eye), as well as colourful lamps, candlesticks, worry beads and Byzantine-style handmade jewellery. After 40 years, the store has relocated upstairs to the 4th floor.
✉ **Voukourestiou 20, Syntagma** ☎ **01 0362 6238** Ⓜ **Syntagma**

### Museum of Cycladic Art Shop (6, E3)

There are many treasures to be found in this impressive gift shop, including exclusive Cycladic figurines and pottery (copied or inspired from the museum's collection) and beautiful books on ancient Greek art.
✉ **Neofitou Douka 4, Kolonaki**
☎ **01 0724 9706**
Ⓜ **Evangelismos**
🕐 **Wed-Fri 10am-4pm, Sat 10am-3pm**

### National Welfare Organisation (9, E6)

Traditional folk art and crafts from all over Greece, including stunning handwoven carpets, kilims, flokatis, tapestries, hand-embroidered

tablecloths, cushion covers and ceramics.
✉ **Ipatias 6 (cnr Apollonos), Plaka**
☎ **01 0321 8272**
Ⓜ **Syntagma**

### Olive Wood (9, E4)

Original creations from half a dozen families in Greece who work exclusively with wood from olive trees – which is so hard it can only be carved, not nailed. The shop has everything from ornaments to wooden spoons to chopping blocks (apparently ideal as the timber is scratch resistant).
✉ **Mnisikleous 8, Plaka**
☎ **01 0321 6145**
Ⓜ **Syntagma**

### Riza (6, D2)

Handmade lace and an extensive range of fabrics for the home, from handblown glass bowls, light fittings and brass candlesticks, to every type of designer kitchen utensil or gadget you might need.
✉ **Voukourestiou 35 (cnr Skoufa), Kolonaki**
☎ **01 0361 1157**
Ⓜ **Syntagma**

*A pensive piece at Takis Moraitis' Plaka gallery & studio*

Neil Setchfield

# MUSIC & BOOKS

**Compendium (9, F8)**
A good selection of new and used books, with popular and quality literature, travel guides, books on Greece and academic publications.
✉ Nikis 28, Plaka
☎ 01 0322 1248
Ⓜ Syntagma

**Eleftheroudakis (9, A9)**
A seven-storey bibliophile's paradise with the widest selection of books from and on Greece, and English-language books, including maps and travel guides. The excellent cafe on the top floor is run by the Food Company.
✉ Panepistimiou 17, Syntagma (& Nikis 20, Plaka) ☎ 01 0331 4180, 01 0331 4183
Ⓜ Syntagma; Panepistimiou
🕐 Mon-Fri 9am-9pm, Sat 9am-3pm

**Metropolis (7, F5)**
A music haven well stocked with local and international CDs, with extensive specialist sections such as dance/hip-hop and progressive rock/post-electronica. The alphabetical listings are a

little confusing. A bigger Greek selection is in the dedicated store further along Panepistimiou.
✉ Panepistimiou 64, Omonia ☎ 01 0383 0804 Ⓜ Omonia
🕐 Mon-Fri 9am-9pm, Sat 9am-6pm

**Nasiotis (9, C1)**
There are literally stacks of old 1st editions, rare books, magazines and engravings along the arcade and in the packed basement, as well as old Greek movie and advertising posters and postcards.
✉ Ifestou 24, Monastiraki
☎ 01 0321 2369
🚇 Monastiraki

**Pandora Music Shop (6, A2)** The place to go for that *bouzouki* or other beautifully hand-crafted traditional Greek instruments, such as the *baglama* (a small bouzouki-style instrument), lutes and tambourines.
✉ Mavromihali 51, Exarhia
☎ 01 0361 9924

Ⓜ Panepistimiou
🕐 Mon, Wed & Sat 11am-3pm, Tues, Thurs & Fri 11am-2pm & 5.30-8pm

**Tzina (7, F5)**
This compact, cramped little store has a good variety of well-categorised music, with some bargains, interesting oddities and best-ofs to be found. One level is dedicated to Greek music, the other to the rest of the spectrum.
✉ Panepistimiou 57, Omonia ☎ 01 0325 1271 Ⓜ Omonia

**Virgin Megastore (9, B9)** There are plenty of headsets at Virgin to listen to the latest releases and a wide selection of Greek CDs and every other sort of music, as well as video games, PlayStations and other toys for big kids.
✉ Stadiou 7-9, Syntagma ☎ 01 0331 4788 Ⓜ Syntagma
🕐 Mon-Fri 9am-9pm, Sat 9am-7pm

*Virgin Megastore*

Neil Setchfield

# FOOD & DRINK

### Aristokratikon (9, C8)
Chocaholics will be delighted by this dazzling array of freshly handmade chocolates including some divine pistachio creations, using the finest ingredients in Greece.
✉ Karagiorgi Servias 9, Syntagma (also in Kifissia) ☎ 01 0322 0546 Ⓜ Syntagma ⏰ Mon-Fri 8am-9pm, Sat 8am-4pm

### Cellier (6, D2)
A wonderful collection of some of the best wines and liqueurs from all over Greece, with highly knowledgable staff to explain the Greek varieties and winemakers. It also sells boxed gift packs.
✉ Kriezotou 1, Syntagma (also in Kifissia) ☎ 01 0361 0040 Ⓜ Syntagma ⏰ Mon-Sat 9am-6pm

### Karavan (6, D2)
A tiny store with rows of sweets and delicious, honey-soaked, nut-filled variations of the baklava, including bite-sized, low-guilt treats.
✉ Voukourestiou 11, Kolonaki ☎ 01 0364 1540 Ⓜ Syntagma ⏰ Mon & Wed 8am-5.30pm, Tues, Thurs & Fri 8am-8.30pm, Sat 8.30am-4pm

### Lysicratous 3 (7, M5)
A great selection of fine Greek wines and spirits, including gift packs, in a delightful, refurbished old Plaka store. The friendly staff can guide you through Greece's unique grape varieties.
✉ Lysikratous 3, Plaka ☎ 01 0323 0350 Ⓜ Syntagma ⏰ Mon-Fri 10am-10pm, Sat 10am-8pm

### Matsouka (9, C9)
Matsouka has huge sacks of nuts and dried fruit (from apricots to mangoes), baked rusks and crusty village bread to cure any

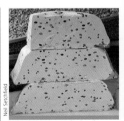
*Take some halva home.*

case of the munchies – and it's open around the clock.
✉ Karagiorgi Servias 3 (cnr Nikis), Syntagma ☎ 01 0325 2054 Ⓜ Syntagma ⏰ 24hrs

### Miseyiannis (6, D3)
A wonderful selection of Greek coffee (and any other type you can imagine), with all the necessary accessories such as a brass briki and special coffee cups.
✉ Leventi 7, Kolonaki ☎ 01 0721 0136 Ⓜ Evangelismos ⏰ Mon, Wed & Sat 7am-3pm, Tues, Thurs & Fri 7am-3pm & 5.30-8.30pm

### Mesogaia (7, L6)
An excellent range of traditional food products from all over Greece, including cheeses, yoghurts and biscuits for immediate consumption. There are also jars of thyme honey with walnuts, *pasteli* (honey and sesame sweets) from Andros, sweets, olives, olive oil and other delectable products to take home.
✉ Nikis 52 (cnr Kydathineon), Plaka ☎ 01 0322 9146 Ⓜ Syntagma ⏰ Mon-Fri 9am-9pm (winter: 9am-8pm), Sat 9am-5pm, Sun 10am-3pm

*A gift for every occasion at the Mesogaia store, Plaka*

# FOR CHILDREN

### Baby Natura (6, D2)
Exquisite clothing and accessories for newborns and young infants, with special christening outfits, bed linen, shoes, toys, nursery decoration and body products – even amulets to guard against the evil eye.
✉ **Milioni 10, Kolonaki**
☎ **01 0361 5494**
Ⓜ **Syntagma**

### Bonbons (3, B3)
Well-made, imported kids clothing in wonderful fabrics and designs for all ages. This spacious, well-ordered store is in a classy sandstone shopping complex.
✉ **Levidou 16, Kifissia**
☎ **01 0808 2993**
🚇 **Kifissia**

### Crocodilino (9, D8)
The shoe fetish in Greece starts at an early age so the selection of kid's shoes is excellent. The extensive range at Crocodilino is Italian-made.
✉ **Voulis 24, Syntagma**
☎ **01 0324 4662**
Ⓜ **Syntagma**

*Kids always smile at a Crocodilino.*

### Gelato (9, C5)
Good-quality children's wear for newborns and children up to 12 years old. Most of the clothing is made in Greece and is well priced.
✉ **Ermou 48, Syntagma** ☎ **01 0322 1777** Ⓜ **Syntagma**

### Kostas Sokaras (9, D1)
Traditional shadow puppets of the legendary folkloric hunchback figure, Karaghiozis, a Greek childhood favourite, and his colourful co-stars in

various sizes are available in this grungy old store.
✉ **Adrianou 25 (near Stoa Attalos), Monastiraki**
☎ **01 0321 6826**
🚇 **Monastiraki**
🕐 **Mon-Fri 9am-1pm**

### Lapin House (9, D7)
This concept store for children's wear, opened by a group of young Greeks nearly 30 years ago, now has stores in Australia, Italy, the Middle East and New York. Excellent quality, stylish clothing for kids of all ages.
✉ **Ermou 21, Syntagma** ☎ **01 0324 1316** Ⓜ **Syntagma**

### Mauve (6, C3)
A unique boutique with old-world charm, Mauve has haute couture babywear, baptismal outfits, bonnets, bibs and sheet sets in lace, lush drapes and a superb selection of antique fabrics.
✉ **Dimokritou 24 (cnr Anagnostopoulou), Kolonaki** ☎ **01 0364 0142** Ⓜ **Evangelismos; Syntagma**
🕐 **closed Aug**

## Beware the Evil Eye
The evil eye is associated with envy, and can be cast – apparently unintentionally – upon someone or something which is praised, coveted or admired (even secretly).

Most culprits are those who are considered peculiar in some way by the locals. Folk with blue eyes are also suspicious; all they have to do is be present when someone or something enviable appears on the scene – and then the trouble starts.

Protection from the evil eye comes from wearing blue or keeping a blue-glass talisman (usually in the shape of an eye) close by. This is a welcome alternative to children or babies (considered especially vulnerable) whose mothers pretend to spit on them to deflect any ill effects.

# SPECIALIST STORES

### Baba (9, C1)
This little hole-in-the wall has been around for ages, selling a small but good range of backgammon sets – a favourite Greek pastime – in all sizes.
✉ **Ifestou 30, Monastiraki**
☎ **01 0321 9994**
🚇 **Monastiraki**

### Filokalia (9, E8)
All manner of ecclesiastical paraphernalia is sold here, including icons, incense, candles, and *tamata* (votive offerings), as well as books on the Greek Orthodox faith.
✉ **Voulis 38, Plaka**
☎ **01 0323 4411**
🚇 **Syntagma**

### Fresh Line (6, D3)
Slabs of exotic natural soaps are sliced from huge blocks and priced by weight in this wonderful store, which has all sorts of lotions, body oils, shampoos and face packs made from unusual combinations of fresh

ingredients. There are also great gift packs.
✉ **Skoufa 10, Kolonaki**
☎ **01 0364 4015**
🚇 **Evangelismos**

### Kamarinos (9, B7)
Kamarinos stocks exquisite antiquarian maps, some dating back to 1500, as well as more than 10,000 faithful reproduction prints from old books and periodicals.
✉ **Kolokotroni 15a, Syntagma** ☎ **01 0323 0923** 🚇 **Syntagma**

### Kaplan Furs (9, D6)
The best furs in Greece are made in the northern Greek city of Kastoria, although the once-thriving industry has suffered from the anti-fur campaigns that have made them most un-PC. Kaplan has a huge selection in all styles.
✉ **Mitropoleos 22-24, Syntagma** ☎ **01 0322 2226** 🚇 **Syntagma**

### Mazarakis (9, E8)
A huge selection of kilims, carpets, rugs and luxurious

traditional Greek flokati rugs that can be packed into surprisingly small parcels to take home – or staff can have them shipped back for you.
✉ **Voulis 31-33, Syntagma** ☎ **01 0323 9428** 🚇 **Syntagma**

### Pylarinos (9, B10)
An undisputed authority on Greek coins and publisher of the definitive Greek numismatic guide spanning 250 years, Pylarinos has stamps dating back to 1828.
✉ **Panepistimiou 18 (in arcade), Syntagma**
☎ **01 0363 0688**
🚇 **Syntagma**

### Thiamis (9, E7)
Iconographer Aristides Makos makes fine hand-painted icons using traditional egg yolk tempera and gold leaf techniques, as well as carved wooden boxes and figurines. Specific patron saints painted to order.
✉ **Apollonos 12, Plaka**
☎ **01 0331 0337**
🚇 **Syntagma**

*Jesus Rocks! Thiamis shop of iconography*

# places to eat

Eating out is a key part of Athenian culture. The Greeks love their food. Fresh local produce, the diversity of regional specialities and creative new takes on traditional dishes offer plenty of delights. A boom in the Athens' culinary scene has seen a proliferation of new restaurants and trendy cafes.

There are options for all palates and budgets, from tasty lamb chops and salad at neighbourhood tavernas to fancy French restaurants and even sushi (although few places have mastered this cuisine).

**Neil Setchfield**

### Meal Costs
The pricing symbols used in this chapter indicate the cost for one person having a two course meal, excluding drinks.

| | |
|---|---|
| $ | under €15 |
| $$ | €15-29 |
| $$$ | €30-47 |
| $$$$ | over €47 |

Old-style casual neighbourhood tavernas are still one of the simple pleasures, and Greeks can do wonders with fish. But Greek cuisine is becoming more sophisticated and the past decade has seen the emergence of upmarket postmodern tavernas, taking traditional flavours and dishes to a new level (and too often the prices as well).

Many restaurants are also bars, which means things liven up after midnight. Most of the restaurants around Plaka and the Acropolis cater to the tourist market, serving standard taverna fare and predictable favourites.

The more contemporary and trendy restaurants close to the city centre are in Psirri, Kolonaki and the up-and-coming former industrial areas around Gazi and Rouf.

Athens has a distinct seasonal dining culture, which means many of the best restaurants will close for the summer, often moving to sister restaurants on the islands. In summer it is all alfresco dining, while winter is an entirely different indoor experience.

### Dining Hours
The first thing you should know about the Athens restaurant scene is that Greeks eat late. Average dinner bookings are at 10pm and it is not uncommon for tables to start filling at midnight. Some of the best restaurants in town don't open until after 9pm, so if you want some atmosphere don't arrive early.

More tourist-friendly eateries open earlier, but if you want to do as the Athenians do, have a late lunch and maybe even sneak in a siesta so you can enjoy things in full swing later on, especially in summer. Reservations are highly recommended for the upper-end restaurants.

DIONYSOS

# ACROPOLIS, MAKRIGIANNI & THISSIO

### Dionyssos-Zonars
(7, M3)    $$

*Greek/International*
Directly opposite the Acropolis, Dionyssos has extensive formal outdoor table seating and a broad menu. This has also become the home of Zonar's Cafe, the Athenian landmark that was forced to move in 2000. Expect to pay top dollar for the coffees.
✉ **Rovertou Gali 43, Makrigianni**
☎ **01 0922 1998**
Ⓜ **Makrigianni**
🕐 noon- 1am; cafe 8am-2pm

### Pil Poul
(8, D8)    $$$$

*Mediterranean/ International*
For a fine dining experience, ambience and a million-dollar view, Pil Poul's rooftop terrace is unsurpassed. This classy 1920s neoclassical mansion frequented by wealthy locals and foreign dignitaries has a modern Mediterranean menu with a strong French influence. Dress up and book ahead.
✉ **Apostolou Pavlou 51 (cnr Poulopoulou), Thissio** ☎ **01 0321 3665** Ⓜ **Thissio; parking available** 🕐 Mon-Sat 8.30pm-1.30am

### Strofi
(7, M3)    $

*Traditional Greek*
This charming taverna has a rooftop terrace with superb Acropolis views and is a regular hang-out of the theatre set after performances at the nearby Herodes Atticus Theatre. Glossy photos on the walls downstairs are testament to its many famous guests. Strofi serves a standard array of quality

*Dionyssos-Zonars restaurant, Makrigianni*

Neil Setchfield

taverna classics at very affordable prices.
✉ **Rovertou Galli 25, Makrigianni** ☎ **01 0921 4130** Ⓜ **Akropoli** 🕐 Mon-Sat 8pm-2am

### Symposio
(7, M3)    $$$

*Modern Greek*
A classy restaurant in a beautifully restored 1920s house, with specialities from north-western Greece. Aside from its signature dish of fish baked in a salt crust, the seasonal menu can include such delicacies as wild boar and pasture-fed yearling beef, wild asparagus, freshwater crayfish, superb mussels and even frogs' legs.
✉ **Erehthiou 46, Makrigianni** ☎ **01 0922 5321** Ⓜ **Akropoli** 🕐 Mon-Sat 8pm-1am

### To Steki tou Ilia
(7, J1)    $

*Taverna/Psistaria*
This is one of the best places in town for meat eaters, with virtual celebrity status (and clients). Lamb chops are sold by the kilogram and grilled to perfection. For variety, there are pork chops and steaks too, as well as a few dips, chips and salads. There are also seats outside in front of the church.
✉ **Thessalonikis 7, Thissio** ☎ **01 0342 2407**

Ⓜ **Thissio** 🕐 Tues-Sun 8pm-1am ♿

### Vithos
(8, C9)    $$

*Greek/Seafood*
A seafood specialist, this stylish corner restaurant spreads to the park across the road for alfresco summer dining with Acropolis views. The pasta dishes are delicious, especially the spaghetti with lobster or langoustines, the grilled fish is excellent, and the wine list offers a decent selection.
✉ **Agion Asomaton 9 (cnr Adrianou), Thissio** ☎ **01 0321 1966** Ⓜ **Thissio** 🕐 noon-2am lunch & dinner

---

## Kid Cuisine

Not many places in Athens have special children's meals or highchairs but most tavernas are children-friendly and it is common to see families out into the wee hours of the night.

Of course the trendier, more upmarket restaurants will not be impressed if you arrive with bratpack in tow, and the hours may be prohibitive in any case.

# GAZI & ROUF

### Aragosta (8, E4) $$
*Mediterranean*
A mix of industrial and island style (complete with ostrich-feather lampshades!) and an eclectic menu make this a popular bar/restaurant. Specialities include rice with red deer on mushrooms and a mean lobster spaghetti. There's a great lounge bar area serving finger food.
✉ Voutadon 58, Gazi
☎ 01 0346 2092
🚖 taxi ⏱ 7pm-1.30am (closed Jul & Aug)

### Aristera-Dexia (8, E3) $$
*Modern Greek/ International*
This super-cool converted car workshop is one of the best restaurants in Athens, with exciting takes on the flavours of the Mediterranean and an excellent

*Ka-ching!*

Neil Setchfield

---

wine list. Style is at a premium here in the decor and presentation. From the novel video-screen entry to the glass cellar to the open kitchen bar – even the toilets are a talking point. Reservations are essential.
✉ Andronikou 3, Rouf
☎ 01 0342 2380
🚖 taxi ⏱ 9pm-1am (closed Jul & Aug) V

### Dirty Fish (8, A5) $$
*Bar/Restaurant*
Modern and refreshing, with a cool design and courtyard in summer, this fish eatery has a mouthwatering range of starters and salads which are all brought out on a tray. The mains, like the rest of the menu, are all seafood and presented in a novel fashion.
✉ Triptolemou 12, Gazi ☎ 01 0347 4763
🚖 taxi ⏱ 9pm-1.30am (Sun lunch) V

### Filistron (8, E9) $$
*Mezedopolio*
A rooftop terrace with Acropolis views makes this a pleasant place for dinner on a warm summer night and the food won't disappoint either. Offerings include a simple, tasty range of meze such as grilled cheese,

---

village-style sausage, meatballs, as well as a selection of greens and salads.
✉ Apostolou Pavlou 23, Thisio ☎ 01 0346 7554 Ⓜ Thissio
⏱ 6pm-late (lunch summer & Sun)

### Interni (8, C9) $$$
*Modern Italian*
Run by the people who have the luxury Italian furniture chain of the same name, Interni is not lacking in fancy design. Good, modern Italian cuisine is accordingly served with style.
✉ Ermou 152, Gazi
☎ 01 0346 8900
🚖 taxi ⏱ Mon-Sat 9pm-1.30am (closed summer) V

### Mamacas (8, B5) $$
*Traditional Greek*
Decked out in cool pastel shades, this Gazi trailblazer puts a modern touch on traditional dishes (cooked, as the name implies, by the owners' mothers). Try the daily specials or staples such as the Mykonian sausage or black-eyed bean salad. Outdoor seating sprawls across the street in summer.
✉ Persefonis 41, Gazi
☎ 01 0346 4984
🚖 taxi ⏱ Mon-Sat 2-6pm & 9pm-1am V

# INNER CITY

### Balthazar (6, A8)   $$$
*Modern Greek*
A summer favourite, in the gorgeous garden of a mansion, Balthazar has huge palm trees and a great bar. The music is not too loud and the crowd cool but not over the top. It's a classy spot with good if slightly overpriced food. The long-awaited opening of the indoor restaurant is pending.
✉ **Tsoha 27 (cnr Vournazou), Ambelokipi**
☎ **01 0644 1215**
Ⓜ **Ambelokipi**
🕓 **9.30pm-1.30am**

### Edodi (7, N3)   $$$$
*Modern Greek/ International*
A tantalising 'live' menu, where waiters parade huge platters of the prepared (yet-to-be cooked) dishes of the day, makes for a truly unique dining experience. The food is clever and creative, not to mention delicious, with a daily selection of nine to ten starters and mains and some wicked desserts. This stylish, tiny restaurant on the 1st floor of a neoclassical building is perfect for a special night out. Reservations are essential.
✉ **Veikou 80, Koukaki**
☎ **01 0921 3013**
Ⓜ **Syngrou-Fix**
🕓 **Mon-Sat 8pm-12.30am**

### Kallimarmaron (7, L9)   $$
*Modern Greek*
Regional specialities with an edge, and excellent seasonal dishes using creative ingredients are complemented by a warm homely atmosphere in this family-run restaurant. Old photos hang on the wall from the time the

*An ohhh... so good aubergine dish, Vlassis restaurant*

family ran the cafe at the old Olympic Stadium nearby.
✉ **Eforionos 13 (cnr Eratosthenous), Pangrati** ☎ **01 0701 9727** 🚌 **2, 11** 🕓 **Mon-Sat lunch & dinner**

### Spondi (7, O9)   $$$
*Modern Greek/ Mediterranean*
This award-winning restaurant in a lovely old Athens mansion has a wonderful ambience and superb courtyard for summer dining. Applauded for its imaginative dishes such as tender pork fillets with *myzithra* cheese in a bittersweet salsa of fig and yogurt, the desserts are also considered among the best in Athens. Reservations are essential.
✉ **Pirronos 5 (off Plateia Varnava), Pangrati** ☎ **01 0756 4021, 01 0752 0658** 🚕 **taxi** 🕓 **8pm-1am**

### Karavitis (7, L9)   $
*Traditional Greek*
A no-frills, old-style taverna with a pleasant garden

courtyard that gets very busy in summer. The barrel wine is drinkable and the food cheap and reliable. It has all the taverna favourites: dips, salads and grilled meats.
✉ **Pafsaniou 4 (cnr Arktinou), Pangrati** ☎ **01 0721 5155** Ⓜ **Evangelismos (plus walk)** 🕓 **8pm-1.30am (garden open May-Oct)** ♿

### Vlassis (6, B8)   $$
*Traditional Greek*
Quality, classic Greek cuisine and a tasteful setting make this one of the best upscale, but modest, tavernas in Athens. An enticing range of starters and favourites such as spinach pie, cabbage *dolmades* and sardines are enough for you to skip the mains and go straight to desserts such as the *halva* (semolina pudding).
✉ **Pasteur 8 (near Plateia Mavili), Ambelokipi** ☎ **01 0646 3060** Ⓜ **Ambelokipi** 🕓 **8.30pm-1am (closed summer)**

# KOLONAKI

## Azul (6, D4) $$

*Modern Greek/ Mediterranean*

In the heart of the happening restaurant and bar strip on the pedestrianised section of Haritos, Azul serves up creative dishes with flare and faultless service. People-watchers will enjoy the outside tables. Reservations are essential.

✉ **Haritos 43**
☎ **01 0725 3817**
Ⓜ **Evangelismos**
🕐 **Mon-Sat 8pm-1.30am**

## Boschetto (6, E6) $$$

*Modern Italian*

In the gardens of Evangelismos Park, Boschetto is one of the most relaxed and classy places to eat in summer and a refreshing escape from the bustle of Athens. The nouvelle Italian cuisine offers some enticing delights and the pasta is the house speciality. There's an extensive range of international and vintage Greek wines.

✉ **Vasilissis Sofias, (Evangelismos Park), Kolonaki** ☎ **01 0721 0893** Ⓜ **Evangelismos**
🕐 **Mon-Sat 8pm-midnight**

## Central (6, D3) $$$

*Modern Greek/ International*

This trendy, semi-underground eatery and lounge bar has won several awards for its food. It's also a great place for a drink or coffee, although it is closed for much of the summer (**Island** is the sister restaurant; see p. 92). It has an excellent selection of wine and spirits, and gets very lively in the evenings.

✉ **Plateia Filikis Eterias 14** ☎ **01 0724 5938** Ⓜ **Evangelismos**
🕐 **lunch & dinner-late**

## Filippou (6, D4) $

*Traditional Greek*

Bookings are recommended at this classic taverna in the Dexameni district, which is always packed with locals enjoying the renowned home-cooked fare at prices rare for this neighbourhood. There's a courtyard and tables on the footpath across the road.

✉ **Xenokratous 19, Kolonaki** ☎ **01 0721 6390** Ⓜ **Evangelismos**
🕐 **lunch & dinner (closed Sat night & Sun)**

## The Food Company (6, D3) $

*Cafe*

Run by a Canadian, this is the only place in town with a range of wholesome ready-made multi-ethnic dishes, including pastas, couscous, curried chicken with rice, Spanish meatballs and delicious roast chicken with rosemary. Great for a casual meal or get takeaway for a picnic. The cakes are equally worth the hike up the hill.

✉ **Anagnostopoulou 47** ☎ **01 0361 6619** Ⓜ **Evangelismos** 🕐 **Mon-Sat 9am-11.30pm (Sun from noon)**

## Gerofinikas (6, D2) $$

*Traditional Greek*

This classic Athenian haunt is popular for business gatherings and is also tourist-friendly. It serves traditional regional specialities such as currant and pine nut pilaf, as well as delicious grilled shrimp with bacon.

✉ **Pindarou 10** ☎ **01 0363 6710** Ⓜ **Syntagma**
🕐 **Mon-Sat noon-1am**

## Jackson Hall (6, D3) $$

*Bar/Restaurant*

This trendy, 3-level bar-cum-restaurant buzzes day and night. American-style burgers and steaks are the speciality, but the seafood pastas are also worth a try. There's a wide selection of beers, ideal people-watching opportunities on the sidewalk and a lively bar scene upstairs.

✉ **Milioni 4**
☎ **01 0361 6098**
Ⓜ **Syntagma**
🕐 **10am-2am**

*The classy Boschetto in the Evangelismos Park*

Neil Setchfield

## Kiku (6, D2)    $$$$
*Japanese*

If you are going to eat Japanese in Athens, then Kiku offers undisputedly the best – and priciest – sushi in town. Ultra stylish and elegant, it has a sushi bar and extensive menu using fresh local fish and imported specialist ingredients. Bookings are advisable.

✉ Dimokritou 12
☎ 01 0364 7033
Ⓜ Syntagma ⏰ Mon-Sat 7.30pm-1am (closed Aug)

## Il Parmigiano (6, C1) $
*Italian*

A large variety of pasta dishes and excellent pizzas make this a popular place for a casual lunch or dinner. With a winning combination of smart design and good food, this has become a reliable Italian chain, with restaurants in Glyfada and Filothei.

✉ Griveon 3
☎ 01 0364 1414
Ⓜ Syntagma
⏰ 1.30pm-2am ⚥

## Prytaneion (6, D3) $$$
*Bar/Restaurant*

This chic restaurant-bar in one of Kolonaki's busy pedestrian thoroughfares has an inviting menu of pasta, seafood and steak dishes and a good selection of wine. There is a pleasant bar for a drink, or sit outside for the free fashion parade.

✉ Milioni 7 ☎ 01 0364 3353-4 Ⓜ Syntagma
⏰ 11am-1am

## Rock'n'Roll (6, E4)   $$
*Bar/Restaurant*

It's the best burger place in town, but that should not suggest the food is

### Greek Wine

Good old retsina has its place, but it has unfortunately done a grave disservice to Greek wine, which is finally beginning to raise its head internationally.

In 2001, a selection of Greek wines got the thumbs up in the *Wine Advocate*, the international industry bible – the first time ever that Greek wine was featured.

There are some wonderful wineries making excellent wines from Greece's unique native grape varieties – reds such as *agiorgitiko* and *xinomavro* and the whites *asyrtiko*, *roditis*, *robola*, *malagouzia* and *moschofilero*.

The industry is becoming more sophisticated as the new generation of winemakers concentrates on producing the best from Greece's climate and varieties. The results are certainly worth a try (see Ⓔ www .greekwine.gr).

unsophisticated – or cheap. It rocks as a bar and is popular with the arts set. Book for dinner and bypass the strict face control, but be warned – the music is loud.

✉ Loukianou 6 (cnr Ipsilantou) ☎ 01 0721 7127 Ⓜ Evangelismos
⏰ 9pm-2am (closed summer)

## To Ouzadiko (6, E4)  $
*Mezedopolio*

Tucked away on the ground-floor atrium of the Lemos Centre, To Ouzadiko offers wonderful traditional meze dishes and seasonal specials in a cosy setting. As the name suggests, there is also an extensive selection of ouzo. Bookings are advisable.

✉ Karneadou 25-29
☎ 01 0729 5484
Ⓜ Evangelismos
⏰ Tues-Sat 1-4pm & 9pm-midnight

## Tutti a Tavola (6, D4)    $$
*Italian*

This stylish semi-basement restaurant serves up great

pastas and Sicilian-style Italian fare in a rustic, warm and relaxed atmosphere. The shellfish pasta is always a winner, as are the mouth-watering truffle risotto and various pasta dishes, washed down with a glass of house wine.

✉ Spefsipou 8 ☎ 01 0725 7756 Ⓜ Evangelismos ⏰ Mon-Sat lunch & dinner-1am

## Zaza (6, C5)        $$
*Bar/Restaurant*

Candy-coloured on the outside and red and pink inside, Zaza certainly makes a bold first impression on the casual observer. But the atmosphere is laid-back and the Australian chefs set this place apart, with creative menus of Mediterranean dishes. The friendly staff and young, hip crowd help make this a fun bar too.

✉ Dinokratous 65, Kolonaki ☎ 01 0722 6430 Ⓜ Evangelismos
⏰ Mon-Sat 9pm-late (brunch Sat & Sun) Ⓥ

# PLAKA & MONASTIRAKI

## Byzantino (7, L6)    $

*Traditional Greek*

One of Plaka's better tavernas, it has traditional cuisine, excellent fish soup and plenty of mageirefta. You can sit outside in the busy square and watch the passing procession. It's good value and popular with locals year-round.

✉ Kydathineon 18, Plaka ☎ 01 0322 7368 Ⓜ Syntagma ⏰ 7am-midnight ⚓

## Café Avyssinia (9, C1)    $

*Music/Mezedopolio*

In the heart of this charmingly grungy Monastiraki square, the action at Café Avyssinia goes on long after the antique and junk dealers have gone home. It's a quirky place with live music and spontaneous floorshows. Best enjoyed on weekend afternoons for a late lunch.

✉ Plateia Avyssinia, Monastiraki ☎ 01 0321 7047 Ⓜ Monastiraki ⏰ closed Mon, Sat & Sun nights

*Tuck into traditional Greek at Platanos, Plaka   .*

## Daphne's (7, L5)    $$

*Mediterranean/ International*

One of the more sophisticated Plaka eateries in an impressive restored neo-classical mansion, Daphne's has frescoes on the walls reminiscent of Pompeii and a courtyard which is pleasant in summer. The menu features regional specialities such as rabbit cooked in mavrodaphne wine and pork cooked with plums.

✉ Lysikratous 4, Plaka ☎ 01 0322 7971, 01 0322 1624 Ⓜ Syntagma, Akropoli ⏰ 7.30-11.45pm

## Orea Ellas (9, D3)    $

*Cafe/Ouzeri*

Escape the madness of Monastiraki by heading upstairs to the ouzeri on the 1st floor of the Centre for Hellenic Tradition. There's a great selection of meze to wash down with ouzo or alternatively coffee and cake. Perfect for a light lunch during shopping or sightseeing expeditions.

✉ Pandrosou 36 or Mitropoleos 59 (Arcade), Monastiraki ☎ 01 0321 3842 Ⓜ Monastiraki ⏰ 9am-8pm

## Ouzeri Kouklis/Scholarheio (7, L5)    $

*Mezedopolio*

There's atmosphere galore at this Plaka institution, an old-style ouzeri with oak-beamed ceilings and marble tables. This was the first schoolhouse in the neighbourhood. Choose from a

## Snack Time

Whether it's the meat on a stick variety, gyros or the spicy mince kebab-style variation on the theme, the *souvlaki* is the best snack in town and you can't leave Athens without trying one. The versions you get overseas just don't compare.

Souvlaki heaven is found in Monastiraki at the end of Mitropoleos, where the unmistakable aromas make it hard to resist. It is packed with diners day and night and the live music, compliments of musicians sitting at one of the tables, gives it a festive feel. **Thanasis'** (9,C3; Mitropoleos 69; ☎ 01 0324 4705; 8.30am-2.30am) is among the best, with special mince kebab-style meat on pitta.

simple but hearty range of mezedes brought out for you on a tray. The house wine is served in plastic bottles.

✉ **Tripodon 14, Plaka**
☎ 01 0324 7605
Ⓜ **Akropoli** ☺ Mon-Fri 9am-3am

### O Damigos/ Bakaliarika (7, L5)   $
*Taverna*
This 1865 basement taverna, reputedly the oldest in Plaka, features in many old Greek movies. It's a lively winter place for traditional Greek fare, just mind your step. The house speciality is *bakaliaro*, salty cod fried in batter, served with lethal garlic dip.

✉ **Kydathineon 41, Plaka** ☎ 01 0322 5084
Ⓜ **Akropoli; Syntagma**

### Eating Late
For a memorable Athens experience after a big night out, go to the darkened central meat market, where the tavernas turn out huge pots and trays of tasty, traditional home-style dishes 24 hrs a day.

An eclectic clientele includes truckies, hungry market workers and elegant couples emerging from local clubs and bars at 5am in search of a bowl of steaming *patsa* (tripe soup) or pig-trotter soup (excellent hangover prevention). Exit as market traders start hanging meat out. Try **Taverna Papandreou** (7, G4; Aristogeitonos 1, Monastiraki; ☎ 01 0321 4970).

### Vegetarian
There are few dedicated vegetarian restaurants in Athens, however most tavernas will have plenty of salads and greens and Greek cuisine is big on vegetable dishes and legumes.

The **Eden Vegetarian Restaurant** (9,F4; Lyssiou 12, Plaka; ☎ 01 0324 8858, Wed-Mon noon-midnight) in Plaka goes unchallenged as the best vegetarian restaurant in town. Soya products are substituted for meat in tasty vegetarian versions of *moussaka* (layers of baked eggplant) and other traditional favourites. It also has vegie burgers and organically produced beer and wine.

☺ 6pm-1am (closed Jul & Aug)

### Palia Taverna tou Psara (9, G4)   $
*Seafood Taverna*
A favourite haunt serving the best and cheapest seafood in Plaka. Recently renovated, the charming old taverna, in a 1898 house in the Anafiotika, retains its great atmosphere and has a pleasant shaded courtyard for those hot summer days.

✉ **Erechteos 16 (cnr Erotokritou), Plaka** ☎ 01 0321 8733
Ⓜ **Monastiraki**
☺ 11am-1am ♿

### Platanos (9, E4)   $
*Traditional Greek*
This age-old taverna with tables in the courtyard under the giant plane tree is popular among Greeks and tourists. It serves delicious home-style fare, such as oven-baked potatoes, lamb fricassee, beef with quince and summer greens. It gets very busy on a summer's night.

✉ **Diogenous 4, Plaka** ☎ 01 0322 0666
Ⓜ **Monastiraki**
☺ Mon-Sat lunch & dinner ♿

### Tade Efi Anna (9, C3)   $$
*American/Mediterranean*
There's a terrace with Acropolis views and an interesting American-style menu with more exotic touches and great starters. In winter, the restaurant moves downstairs to a bright new modern space with warm colours and unique light fittings.

✉ **Ermou 72, Monastiraki**
☎ 01 0321 3652
Ⓜ **Monastiraki**
☺ Mon-Sat 9pm-1.30am

### To Kouti (9, D1)   $$
*Modern Greek*
Some outside tables have an Acropolis view but if you miss out the food at this recently renovated, popular eatery is adequate consolation. The cute Greek menus are handwritten in children's books but plain English versions will help you select from a creative menu, with great salads and desserts.

✉ **Adrianou 23, Thisio** ☎ 01 0321 3229
Ⓜ **Thissio** ☺ noon-2am lunch & dinner

# OMONIA & EXARHIA

### Athinaikon (7, F5)    $
*Mezedopolio*

An institution in central Athens, it offers a wide selection of traditional meze and seafood dishes such as fried calamari or rice with mussels. The marble-top tables, old-style atmosphere (it's been around since 1932) and friendly service make this a popular place.

✉ Themistokleous 2 (cnr Panepistimiou), Omonia ☎ 01 0383 8485 Ⓜ Omonia ⏰ Mon-Sat 11.30-1am (closed Aug)

*Athinaikon – the place to go for that traditional Greek experience*

### Diporto (7, G3)    $
*Mezedopolio*

Go back in time with this quirky underground taverna near the Athens Central Food Markets. There is no signage, only two doors leading to the basement where there's no menu, just a few dishes that haven't changed in years (such as chickpeas and grilled fish), washed down with the only wine – *retsina* (resinated white wine).

✉ Theatrou 1 (cnr Sofokleous), Omonia Ⓜ Omonia ⏰ Mon-Sat 8am-7pm

### Bar Guru Bar (7, G3)    $$
*Thai*

For a spicy night out this busy bar/restaurant near Athens fruit and vegetable market has an excellent Thai menu, funky decor, great music (late) and a hip crowd. It's a little hard to find, but Thai food is a rarity in Athens.

✉ Plateia Theatrou 10, Omonia ☎ 01 0324 6530 Ⓜ Omonia ⏰ 9pm-1.30am (closed Jul & Aug)

### Klimataria (7, G3)    $
*Music Taverna*

This no-frills, old-style tavern located near the Central Food Market is like taking a step back in time, with a great atmosphere and decent, basic traditional mezedes. There's live Greek music on most nights, including a fantastic line-up of old-timers, led by the octogenarian viloninst Arapakis, playing rebetika and various music from Smyrna.

✉ Plateia Theatrou 2, Omonia ☎ 01 0321 6629 Ⓜ Omonia ⏰ Mon-Sat 12.30pm-2am (& Sun lunch)

### The Olive Garden (7, F5)    $$
*Mediterranean*

The Titania hotel's roof garden has Acropolis views and a pleasant cocktail bar. However, it is the food that stands out, with quality Greek and Mediterranean cuisine and some interesting Asian accents. The octopus with prawns with Sambuca are excellent.

✉ Panepistimiou 52, Omonia ☎ 01 0383 8511 Ⓜ Omonia ⏰ lunch & dinner-1am

### Taverna Rozalia (7, E7)    $
*Traditional Greek*

Rozalia is a family-run taverna with a standard menu and a huge courtyard garden. It's located off the pedestrian thoroughfare in Exarhia. Excellent value grilled meats, salads and house wine ensure it is always busy.

✉ Valtetsiou 58, Exarhia ☎ 01 0330 2933 🚕 taxi ⏰ noon-2am ♿

### Yiantes (7, E7)    $
*Modern Greek*

Yiantes is a little oasis next to the Riviera open-air cinema, with trees towering over a delightful colourful courtyard, and funky retro decor inside. Creative regional specialities from all over Greece are on offer with contemporary touches and ample servings. Try the Byzantine pork with coriander or wild pig in *mavrodaphne* (red wine) sauce.

✉ Valtetsiou 44, Exarhia ☎ 01 0330 1369 🚕 taxi ⏰ noon-2am

# PSIRRI

### Avalon (8, B9)    $$
*Bar/Restaurant*
The atmosphere is part-Greek part-medieval, but the mussels are the main attraction, cooked with almost any spice and sauce (there are 13) you can imagine. The pleasant courtyard roof opens in summer, but this is a popular place year-round.
✉ Leokoriou 20 (cnr Sarri) ☎ 01 0331 0572 🚊 Thissio ⏲ Tues-Sun 8pm-late (Sun from noon)

### Kouzina (8, B9)    $$
*Modern Greek/Mediterranean*
Right next to the popular Cine Psirri outdoor cinema, this former factory has a warm atmosphere, friendly service and a creative menu. There's an impressive glass floor revealing the cellar, and a rooftop terrace with Acropolis views.
✉ Sarri 40 ☎ 01 0321 5534 🚊 Thissio; Monastiraki
⏲ Tues-Sat 9pm-1am, Sun 2pm-1am; summer: Mon-Sat

### To Krasopoulio tou Kokkora (9, B1)    $
*Mezedopolio*
Once an historic music taverna, the restaurant is decorated with appropriate collectables and old newspaper clippings. The tradition continues with live music every night and during Sunday lunch. The house speciality is chicken, grilled to perfection, and the salads are excellent.
✉ Esopou 4 (cnr Karaiskaki) ☎ 01 0321 1051 🚊 Monastiraki ⏲ 1pm-late

### Methystanes (8, B10)    $$
*Modern Greek*
In a gorgeous restored two-level neoclassical building, this lively restaurant has excellent food (try the potato souffle) and a duo playing great *entekna* music and popular favourites. Worth going late for a drink and snack at the bar.
✉ Lepeniotou 26 (cnr Ogigou) ☎ 01 0331 4298 🚊 Monastiraki; Thissio ⏲ Tues-Sat 8.30pm-late

### Plateia Iroon (9, A1)    $
*Mezedopolio*
A popular meeting spot in the heart of Psirri, with great taverna classics and a casual atmosphere. There's outdoor seating on Plateia Iroon, and a cosy interior with music after 9pm every night.
✉ Karaiskaki 34 ☎ 01 0321 1915 🚊 Monastiraki ⏲ 2pm-2am

### Taki 13 (9, A1)    $
*Music Taverna/Mezedopolio*
This three-venue restaurant (don't do a double-take) was the first music taverna to open in Psirri and has a tradition of lively Sunday afternoons. The range of meze is fairly standard and the service can be slow, but Psirri is not the place to go if you are in a hurry.
✉ Taki 13 ☎ 01 0325 4707 Ⓜ Monastiraki ⏲ daily for dinner (Fri-Sun lunch) ♿

### To Zeidoron (9, A1)    $
*Mezedopolio*
One of the Psirri originals, it has tables outside across from Agion Anargiron church, where you can watch the passing promenade. There is a variety of meze starters and interesting daily specials. It has a cosy interior for the winter.
✉ Agion Anargiron 17 (cnr Taki) ☎ 01 0321 5368 🚊 Monastiraki ⏲ 10am-2am

---

### Psirri On Line
The innovative Web site ⓔ www.psirri.gr has a useful directory of galleries, restaurants and happenings in Psirri.

*A simply scrumptious starter to your meal.*

# SYNTAGMA & THE CENTRE

## Aigli Bistrot
(7, L7) **$$$**
*Mediterranean Cafe/ Restaurant*
It's not just the setting in the Zappeio Gardens that makes this a great choice for summer or winter. Aigli has a fine menu of high standard, simple dishes presented with flair, as well as an extensive wine list. There are live outdoor jazz performances in summer.
✉ **Zappeio Gardens, Zappeio** ☎ **01 0336 9363-4** Ⓜ **Syntagma**
🕐 **1-4pm & 8.30pm-12.30am**

## Aiolis (9, B4) **$**
*Bar/Restaurant*
Tucked in a pedestrian way, off the busy Ermou shopping strip, Aiolis is a great daytime pit-stop. It has tables under the trees on the sidewalk, next to the Church of Agia Irini, and serves nice pasta dishes, snacks and a good range of coffee, tea and milk shakes. It gets lively at night, occasionally with live music.
✉ **Eolou 23 (cnr Ag. Irinis), Monastiraki** ☎ **01 0331 2839** 🚊 **Monastiraki**
🕐 **10am-2am**

## Cellier Le Bistrot (9, B10) **$$**
*Greek/International*
A newcomer to the Athens restaurant scene run by one of the leading wine merchants, Cellier is one of the few places with an extensive selection of Greek wines by the glass. It has an international feel and menu, with a choice of salads and lighter meals. Great for lunch.
✉ **Panepistimiou 10 (in Arcade), Syntagma** ☎ **01 0363 8525** Ⓜ **Syntagma**
🕐 **noon-1am**

## Furin Kazan (9, E8) **$$**
*Japanese*
Japanese tourists fill this casual, cafe-style restaurant before a second shift of late-night Greek diners descend. The service is not always friendly, but the food makes up for it – quality sushi and sashimi, as well as some delicious noodle dishes.
✉ **Apollonos 2, Syntagma** ☎ **01 0322 9170** Ⓜ **Syntagma**
🕐 **Mon-Sat 11am-11pm**

## Palia Vouli (9, B8) **$$**
*Mediterranean/Italian*
Set in a cool, green corner of Athens, next to the old Parliament building (thus the name), it has an old-world feel, with lit-up fountain and a piano that would make Liberace proud. There's a reasonable menu of fresh pasta and Italian-style dishes.
✉ **Anthimou Gazi 9 (cnr Karitsi)** ☎ **01 0331 4773** Ⓜ **Syntagma**
🕐 **8am-2am**

*'Pass the dolmades'*

Alan Benson

# CAFES & SWEET TREATS

Having coffee seems to be the national pastime, so there is no shortage of places to go. Old-style coffee houses serving Greek coffee are becoming rarer these days. DeCapo in the coffee-mecca square on Kolonaki has the reputation for the best coffee in town, but if you can't get a seat there are plenty of options around the square on nearby Milioni, not to mention the rest of town.

### Dodoni (6, D3) $
*Cafe*
Which flavour? Ice-cream connoisseurs will love the unique Greek ice creams at this leading chain, along with all the wicked toppings.
✉ Milioni 9, Kolonaki
☎ 01 0363 7387
Ⓜ Syntagma
🕐 8am-2am ⚕

### Filion (6, C2) $
*Cafe*
Casual, airy and open, you can sit and enjoy the luscious cakes that line the long glass display cabinet. On Saturdays you can even watch the weddings at the church next door.
✉ Skoufa 34, Kolonaki
☎ 01 0361 2850
Ⓜ Syntagma
🕐 8am-1am ⚕

### Klepsidra (9, F3) $
*Cafe/Sweets*
A cosy cafe with a terrace overlooking the Anafiotika in Plaka, it has home-made Greek sweets (try the walnut pie with ice cream) and speciality dairy products. The *spanakopita* (spinach pie) is served with a dollop of fresh yogurt and there are treats such as iced mountain tea.
✉ Plaka ☎ 01 0321 8726 🚇 Monastiraki
🕐 summer: 9am-2am; winter: 10am-11pm ⚕

### Kotsolis (7, K4) $
*Cafe/Sweets*
Founded in 1906, the Kotsolis family continue their

late father's tradition, making delicious pastries such as *galaktoboureko* (custard pastry), rice puddings and *loukoumades* (Greek-style doughnuts). Also sells gift packs of honeys and sweets.
✉ Adrianou 112, Plaka
☎ 01 0322 1164
🚇 Monastiraki
🕐 9am-late ⚕

### Melina (9, F4) $
*Cafe*
A quaint cafe, Melina is dedicated to Greece's legendary actress and politician, the late Melina Mercouri. There's interesting memorabilia and photographs, china tea sets and a cosy yet formal, old-world style.
✉ Lyssiou 22, Plaka
☎ 01 0324 6501
🚇 Monastiraki
🕐 noon-late

### O Kipos (7, K8) $
*Cafe*
A little oasis in the back of the National Gardens, this is a popular spot for locals and tourists seeking relief from the heat and bustle in summer. As well as coffees and refreshments there is a basic selection of sandwiches and light snacks.
✉ Herodou Attikou, National Gardens
Ⓜ Syntagma 🕐 10am-sunset ⚕

### To Tristrato (7, L6) $
*Cafe*
This little gem off Plaka's busy square specialises in desserts made from milk

such as galaktoboureko and rice pudding. It has a wonderful traditional feel and a great selection of herbal and mountain teas.
✉ cnr Aggelou Geronta & Dedalou, Plaka ☎ 01 0324 4472 Ⓜ Syntagma
🕐 Mon-Fri 11am-1pm, Sat-Sun from 10am (closed Aug) ⚕

*Strong Greek coffee – a national institution.*

### Varsos (3, B2) $
*Patisserie/Cafe*
A landmark in Kifissia, this huge patisserie has been making high-quality traditional Greek sweets and dairy products since 1892. Walk past the trays of goodies to the old-style cafe or sit in the outside courtyard and try the fresh rice pudding, honeyed pastries, yogurt or scrumptious cheese pies, and the best value coffee in Kifissia.
✉ Kassaveti 5, Kifissia
☎ 01 0801 3743
🚇 Kifissia
🕐 7am-late ⚕

# WORTH THE TRIP

### Beau Brummel
(3, C2) $$$$

*French*

Formal dining at its best, Beau Brummel has received international recognition for its tasteful decor, exceptional service and excellent quality food. There's a €44 set menu downstairs. Bookings are essential.

✉ **Agiou Dimitriou 9 (cnr Agion Theodoron), Kifissia**
☎ **01 0623 6780**
🚖 **taxi**
🕐 **Mon-Sat noon-4.30 & 8pm-1am**

### Dourambeis (5, D8) $$
*Seafood Taverna*

An enduring seafront taverna in Piraeus, you can get fresh fish here grilled to perfection and served with a simple oil and lemon dressing, as well as wonderful crayfish soup.

✉ **Akti Protopsalti 27, Piraeus** ☎ **01 0412 2092** 🚖 **taxi**
🕐 **lunch & dinner**

There's nothing fishy about the catch of the day here.

### Jimmy & the Fish
(5, D8) $$$

*Seafood*

It's hard to go past the lobster spaghetti and other seafood pastas which are house specialities, along with an excellent daily catch of fresh fish. One of the more stylish places among the fish tavernas that line Mikrolimano, Jimmy's has a great range of entrees, including stuffed calamari, and ouzo and sesame prawns.

✉ **Akti Koumoundourou 46, Mikrolimano, Piraeus**
☎ **01 0412 4417**
🚖 **taxi** 🕐 **12.30pm-1.30am**

Gefsis me Onomasies Proelefsis restaurant, Kifissia

Neil Setchfield

### Gefsis me Onomasies Proelefsis
(3, A2) $$$

*Modern Greek*

A stylish restaurant in a renovated neoclassical mansion, it specialises in traditional dishes based on regional ingredients, all prepared with a sophisticated, modern touch. It has an excellent wine list and an extensive range of Greek cheeses.

✉ **Kifissias 317, Kifissia** ☎ **01 0800 1402** 🚖 **taxi** 🕐 **Mon-Sat lunch & dinner**

### Istioploikos
(5, D8) $$$

*Seafood*

The restaurant is on a moored restored ship at the western end of Mikrolimano Harbour, with great views and a stunning bar on the top level open for drinks until late. Fresh seafood is creatively presented on an international-style menu.

✉ **Akti Mikrolimanou, Piraeus** ☎ **01 0413 4084** 🚖 **taxi** 🕐 **lunch & dinner-1am**

### Lambros
(1, E4) $$$

*Seafood taverna*

Founded in 1889 during the reign of King George I,

Lambros was cooking fish when seaside Vouliagmeni was a day trip from Athens. The expanded, upmarket restaurant of today, right on the water, is still a favourite Sunday lunch spot for Athenians.
✉ **Poseidonos 20 (opposite Limni Vouliagmenis), Vouliagmeni** ☎ **01 0896 0144** 🚕 taxi ⏱ lunch & dinner

**Sphinx (4, C5)**    **$$$**
*Modern Mediterranean*
It's not by the water, but the garden courtyard is a cool place in summer, with Mediterranean fusion-style cuisine. There's usually live music on Thursday night.
✉ **Kiprou 65a, Glyfada** ☎ **01 0894 0050** 🚕 taxi ⏱ **Mon-Sat 8.30pm-1.30am**

**Ta Kioupia (1, B4)**    **$$$**
*Modern/Traditional Greek*
Ta Kioupia is a smorgasbord covering the spectrum of Greek cuisine, from island influences, regional specialities, and modern and classic dishes. The setting is impressive and there is a cheaper set menu, as well as a la carte dining.
✉ **Plateia Politias, Kifissia** ☎ **01 0620 0005** 🚕 taxi ⏱ **Mon-Sat lunch & dinner (Sun lunch only)**

**Thalassinos (1, D3)**    **$$**
*Seafood*
Inconspicuously tucked away in a residential street behind the Onassis Cardiac Centre, Thalassinos has some of the most interesting seafood in town. The eclectic menu includes smoked fish nibbles,

> ## Great Views
> For the ultimate romantic evening with views of the illuminated Acropolis, you can't beat **Pil Poul** (p. 75), or the less extravagant alternative, **Strofi** (p. 75).
>
> For a seaside dinner, head to **Istioploikos** (p. 86) in Piraeus, where you can dine (or just have a drink) on a huge boat-turned-restaurant overlooking Mikrolimano Harbour (below).

Neil Setchfield

*Chew on this view from a harbourside eatery.*

inventive dips, vegetable and seafood fritters and sublime calamari with pesto.
✉ **Lysikratous 32 (cnr Irakleous), Tzitzifies** ☎ **01 0940 4518** 🚕 taxi ⏱ **Mon-Sat 8.30pm-1am (closed Aug)**

**Vardis (3, A5)**    **$$$$**
*Modern French/ Mediterranean*
With a claim to Greece's only Michelin star, Vardis is the big splurge in Athens' gastronomic scene. Located in the lovely Pentelikon hotel, its food and service are exquisite, although the jury is out on the impact of the defection

of its winning chef to Beau Brummel.
✉ **Diligianni 66, Kefalari** ☎ **01 0628 1660** 🚕 taxi ⏱ **Mon-Sat 8pm-12.30am (closed Aug)**

**Varoulko (5, B7) $$$$**
*Seafood/Mediterranean*
Book ahead for a seafood lover's treat at this classic Piraeus taverna. Choose from an imaginative range of daily specials or specialities such as crab salad with mango and grapes, mullet roe or the chef's many variations on monkfish.
✉ **Deligiorgi 14, Piraeus** ☎ **01 0422 1283** 🚕 taxi ⏱ **Mon-Sat 8pm-1am**

# ententertainment

If there's one thing Greeks pride themselves on, it's their ability to have a good time. A few years back, the government tried to impose stricter closing times on nightclubs to boost the country's productivity, but a virtual rebellion put a stop to that and Athenians now happily party to all hours.

There is a tremendous range of bars, music venues and clubs to suit most musical tastes, from rock to jazz to Greek pop and folk music. Greek music is alive and well in all its contemporary and traditional forms, but Athens also hosts rock and blues festivals, gets some impressive big-name international acts and in 2001 hosted its first Womad festival.

The highlight of the cultural calendar is the annual Athens Festival, which brings leading performers, orchestras and dance troupes from around the world. The Cultural Olympiad will ensure a major program of special events takes place in the lead up to the 2004 Olympics.

There is also a thriving theatre tradition, both mainstream and experimental, but given the performances are in Greek, theatre has not been emphasised here. For club-

## What to Wear?

Athenians like to dress up for a night out and the more stylish the place, the more you are likely to feel uncomfortable if you rock up looking like a backpacker. In the really upmarket bars and clubs, which have strict 'face control', you may get turned away at the door, especially if you are in a big group of men. Dress to impress.

Tavernas, bars and restaurants in tourist areas are more casual but smart casual wear is recommended.

bers, Athens offers a vibrant dance club scene with more stamina than most cities in the world – the clubs often only start filling after 3am.

As with restaurants, the entertainment scene starts late and most clubs would be empty before midnight. Going out is not cheap, and even if there is no door charge, rest assured the drinks bill will make up for it (although the serves are usually doubles).

## Before you Dial

Greece is in the process of entirely changing its phone numbering system – of course it is being done in a couple of stages just to make it more confusing. So before you pick up the phone to make that booking, check the telephone information on p. 116.

The phone numbers listed in this book are valid until October 2002.

Pick your poison at this popular Plaka bar – Brettos, Plaka.

Neil Setchfield

## SPECIAL EVENTS

**6 January** *Epiphany* – the blessing of the water takes place in Piraeus, where young men dive in to retrieve a cross thrown into the sea. The winner is blessed with good luck for the year.

**February** *Apokries* – the Greek Carnivale, when fancy-dress parties are held all over town

*Votive offerings at a local church*

**February/March** *Ash Monday* – at the beginning of Lent, Athenians fly kites on Filopappou Hill, Lykavittos Hill and parks around the city

**25 March** *Greek National Day* – full military parade in the city along Akadimias every second year (schools parade on alternate years)

**March/April** *Easter* – night church services including a candlelit procession on Good Friday and midnight services on Easter Saturday

**May** *Spring* – the arrival of spring is celebrated by going to mountains and collecting wildflowers to make wreaths, which are hung in doorways

**June-September** *Athens Festival* – music, dance and drama in venues around Athens, the biggest being the Athens Festival (see p. 95)

*Epidauros Festival* – ancient Greek drama festival at the ancient Theatre of Epidauros (see p. 95)

**July** *Rockwave* – Greece's biggest annual rock music festival, with three days of non-stop music by some top international acts. For information: **e** www.didimusic .gr/rockwave.htm. Tickets from TicketHellas ☎ 01 0618 9300.

**28 October** *Ohi Day* – military parade, celebrating the rejection of the Italian ultimatum in 1940

*Ensure good luck for the year by catching the cross at this ritual held on the Epiphany.*

# BARS & CLUBS

There is always something happening in Athens but there are two distinct seasons and styles of entertainment. In winter the liveliest bars are in Kolonaki, Psirri, Gazi and the inner-city area.

**Banana Moon (7, M8)**
Right next to the old Olympic Stadium, Banana Moon spills out onto the footpaths in summer. It's open all day but comes into its own at night, with a resident DJ and regular procession of well-heeled Athenians.
✉ Agras & Vasileos Konstantinou, Mets (next to Stadium)
☎ 01 0752 1768
Ⓜ Syntagma
🚌 2, 11, 14
🕙 10am-late

**Barfly (8, B5)**
A stylish bar and restaurant that gets lively late, with a young and not-too-young mainstream crowd. There's imaginative cuisine – and music – catering to all tastes, and a great view over Gazi.
✉ Voutadon 34, Gazi
☎ 01 0346 0347
🚕 taxi 🕙 9pm-late

**Brettos (7, L5)**
A Plaka landmark, this quaint little bar has a stunning backlit wall of coloured bottles, old wine barrels along another wall and a refreshingly old-fashioned feel. It's a spirits shop by day and a quiet spot for a nightcap later on.
✉ Kydathineon 41, Plaka ☎ 01 0323 2110
Ⓜ Syntagma
🕙 10am-midnight

**Briki (6, B8)**
This tiny bar gets so busy the crowd spills out on to Plateia Mavili. It's one of Athens' biggest night-time drinking holes, where revellers from adjoining bars meet around the fountain. If you get the late-night munchies, the hot-dog stands park here at night.
✉ Dorileou 6, Plateia Mavili, Ambelokipi
☎ 01 0645 2380
Ⓜ Ambelokipi
🕙 9pm-late

**Café Folie (6, A9)**
A cosy, established and popular bar with colourful, funky decor, Folie attracts a mixed and friendly crowd, with music ranging from reggae to ethnic. Things get lively late but if you need more space, head next door to Folie's full-on dance club.
✉ Eslin 4, Ambelokipi
☎ 01 0646 9852
Ⓜ Ambelokipi
🕙 10.30am-late (club: Mon-Sat 11pm-late)

**Cubanita Havana Club (7, H3)**
Latin music is so 'in' there's more chance of doing the salsa than the Zorba these days. Cubanita has great live acts and DJs spinning the latest Latin tunes. There's pricey Cuban food and a large selection of cigars. The bar moves to a huge waterfront venue in Glyfada in summer.
✉ Karaiskaki 28, Psirri
☎ 01 0331 4605
🚇 Monastiraki
🕙 Mon-Sat 9.30pm-3am, Sun 5pm-2am
⑤ €8.80

**De Luxe (7, N5)**
Funky 60s-airport decor, an innovative menu and a very alternative young crowd make this a fun place for a drink or a meal. A great mix of music and a friendly bar team.
✉ Falirou 15, Makrigianni
☎ 01 0924 3184
Ⓜ Akropoli
🕙 9pm-late (dinner till 1.30am)

**Fidelio (8, B10)**
A great space with lots of stone and wood, the front

*Skoufaki – a casual cafe in Kolonaki*

Neil Setchfield

bar opens completely in summer, with bar stools on the footpath and crowds spilling onto the street. The music ranges from soul/funk to electronica to blues – depending on the DJ.

✉ **Ogigou 2 (cnr Navarhou Apostoli), Psirri** ☎ 01 0321 2977
🚇 Thissio
🕑 9.30pm-3.30am

### Antico Theatro (1, D2)
This romantic beachfront bar-restaurant takes you virtually into the water. The former summer palace of King Otto and Amalia is decked out in white, contrasting beautifully with the sea. You pay for the view.

✉ **Poseidonos (opposite 33), Palio Faliro** ☎ 01 0981 4245
🚖 taxi 🕑 9pm-late
💲 €8.80 Fri & Sat

### Inoteka (9, C1)
You might wonder what you are doing as you head down the dark alley towards the deserted Monastiraki Flea Market, but persevere and you will find a casual, candlelit bar, playing great freestyle music. If you stay out late enough, you will meet the traders setting up for the Sunday market.

✉ **Plateia Avyssinias 3, Monastiraki** ☎ 01 0324 6446 🚇 Monastiraki
🕑 1pm-late

### Mike's Irish Bar
(6, B9) Mike's not Irish but you can still hear live Irish music, as well as classic rock and blues most nights. There's Guinness on tap and a mixed crowd.

✉ **Sinopis 6, Athens Tower, Ambelokipi** ☎ 01 0777 6797

---

🚌 13 🕑 8pm-late
💲 €2.93 for live bands

### Skoufaki (6, C2)
This cosy bar is great for a coffee and snack or a quiet drink during the day. In the evening it livens up with a more upbeat trendy crowd. It's a casual meeting place, with cool music.

✉ **Skoufa 47-49, Kolonaki**
☎ 01 0364 5888
🚇 Syntagma 🕑 11am-3am (later Fri & Sat)

### Stavlos (8, D8)
A happening bar and restaurant in the old Royal stables, the highlight is the internal courtyard, which is green and cool. It is also a popular alternative rock venue, although it attracts all ages. There are tables outside if the music gets too much or you prefer to check out the passing crowd.

✉ **Iraklidon 10, Thisio**
☎ 01 0346 7206
🚇 Thissio 🕑 10am-4am

### Stoa (7, A5)
An old shopping arcade has been turned into a multipurpose venue with a restaurant and two bars, each with their own feel. The central bar and open space allows for a quieter drink, while the swinging bar has mainstream music and a mixed, casual crowd.

✉ **Patission 101 & Kodringtonos, Pedion**

---

**Areos** ☎ 01 0825 3932
🚌 3, 11, 13 🚇 Victoria
🕑 Tues-Sun lunch & dinner till late
💲 €5.87 door charge (inc 1st drink)

### Tango (9, A1)
This spacious, two-level bar-restaurant is a popular place to eat, meet and drink, with tables in the square across the road. The crowd is congenial and the music mainstream. In summer, the action moves down to the beach at Voula (Alkionidon 4; ☎ 01 0895 6577).

✉ **Agion Anargyron 21-23, Psirri**
☎ 01 0331 1992
🚇 Thissio 🕑 until late

### Thirio (8, B10)
A two-level warren of small rooms, lounges and bar-drinking spots, the Lilliputian Thirio (Greek for giant) is funky and fun, and the music ranges from acid jazz to ethnic. It can get very crowded.

✉ **Lepeniotou 1, Psirri**
☎ 01 0722 4104
🚇 Monastiraki
🕑 9pm-late

### Vibe (9, A1)
Minimalist Japanese-style is the go at this cool bar, with regular guest DJs, freestyle music and wild zebra-print seats. It rocks late.

✉ **Aristofanous 1 (Plateia Iroon), Psirri**
☎ 01 0324 4794
🚇 Monastiraki
🕑 Tues-Sun till late

# SUMMER BARS & CLUBS

In summer, people prefer to be outdoors so the many winter venues close (unless they have a garden or outdoor seating) and the action moves to outdoor bars at the seaside in Piraeus, Glyfada and along the coast. Kifissia and the northern suburbs also have many good bars and nightclubs.

### Bedlam (7, L7)

A stunning new summer bar in the middle of the Zappeio Gardens, with lime-cushion lounges, pop art on the walls and crystals hanging from the trees. There's multi-ethnic finger food and a cool crowd.
✉ **Zappeio Gardens, Syntagma** ☎ **01 0336 9340-1** Ⓜ **Syntagma**
🕒 **9pm-late**

### Exo (7, N7)

A popular bar in summer, with a rooftop terrace and great views of the Acropolis and Lykavittos Hill. House music, sushi and a hip mixed-age crowd make this one of the trendiest city venues. Reserve one of the private lounge areas on the veranda or brave it with the throng.
✉ **Markou Mousourou 1, Mets**
☎ **01 0923 5818**
🚌 **2, 11, 14 from Syntagma** 🕒 **9pm-late**
💲 **€11.70 Fri & Sat**

### Budha (4, A1)

A popular and classy beach-side club with a huge pool and bar that operates day and night. It has a Miami/Greek island feel and a cool crowd to match – plus the flashiest bikinis in town.
✉ **Diadohou Pavlou 20, Glyfada** ☎ **01 0894 4048** 🚕 **taxi**
🕒 **9.30am-late**
💲 **€8.80 Mon-Thurs; €11.70 Fri & Sat**

### Island (1, E4)

A beautiful seaside club, with Cycladic island decor and an ultra-glam crowd. It's a long way to go to be turned away by the 'face control' – booking for dinner is your best bet, then stay on for a drink before the music is turned up.
✉ **Limanakia Vouliag-menis, Varkiza** ☎ **01 0965 3563-4** 🚕 **taxi**
🕒 **midnight-late**

### On the Road (7, N7)

This long and narrow bar 'on the road' is a patch of

### Shutdown

Athens' club scene has traditionally moved to the beach in summer to huge open-air venues that rock all night. Many were illegally constructed on the beach and were served closure notices; others are in areas earmarked for the construction of Olympic facilities. It was unclear at the time of research which clubs would reopen in the summer of 2002.

green between two busy thoroughfares. It turns into a happening bar at night, with cosy corners and full-on dance areas with guest DJs and the latest club music.
✉ **Ardittou 1, Mets**
☎ **01 0347 8716**
🚌 **2, 11,14**
🕒 **10pm-late**
💲 **€8.80 Fri & Sat**

## Beer, Beer & More Beer

There aren't many English-style pubs in Greece but **Craft Athens** (6, A9; Alexandras 205, Ambelokipi; ☎ 01 0646 2350; Sun-Fri 10am-1.30am, Sat 10am-2am) is a full-on microbrewery where you can sit among the industrial machinery that brews six different beers, including an ale called 'Swedish Blonde'.

It's a huge multilevel complex – downstairs looks like the set of *Star Trek*. There's a restaurant serving international cuisine ranging from Asian to Tex-Mex and you can join in on the fun with tours and tastings on Thursday at 10pm.

# DANCE CLUBS

### Envy (3, A5)
Ultra-modern design and an ultra-cool attitude to match, this club in busy Kefalari Square attracts the glam crowd but the 'face control' is strict. It's often lively on Sunday afternoons. In summer, Envy moves to Voula beach.
✉ **Deligianni 50, Kefalari/Kifissia** ☎ **01 0801 8304** 🚇 **Kifissia** ⊘ **Wed-Sat 11pm-5am, Sun 7pm-2am** ⑤ **€5.87/11.74 Fri/Sat**

### Kalua (9, A10)
A classic downtown club with house music (and occasional Greek club music), where there is usually pandemonium. Oriental decor features, as does an under 30s crowd. The club moves to Alimo beach in summer.
✉ **Amerikis 6, Syntagma** ☎ **01 0360 8304** Ⓜ **Syntagma** ⊘ **11.30pm-late** ⑤ **€8.80 Sun-Thurs, €11.74/14.67 Fri/Sat**

### Lava Bore (7, L6)
A popular tourist hangout, where locals go to brush up on their *kamaki* (pick-up) techniques. It's a casual bar, close to Plaka. The music is mainstream and retro, but the place can be tacky.
✉ **Filellinon 25, Syntagma** ☎ **01 0324 5335** Ⓜ **Syntagma** ⊘ **10.30pm-late**

### Plus Soda (8, C6)
A multilevel club with huge dance floor, and a regular line-up of guest DJs. One for young, hardcore clubbers, the music is

*Pop in for a soda.*

progressive/psychedelic trance, house and techno – and the lights and pace are not for the faint-hearted.
✉ **Ermou 161, Thisio** ☎ **01 0345 6187** 🚇 **Thissio** ⊘ **Wed-Sun till late** ⑤ **€11.74 (more for special guest DJ performances)**

### Prime (7, N6)
One of the bigger, established and trendy clubs, with mainstream music and crowds of all ages, not to mention the scantily clad dancers on podiums. After 3am, there's live Greek music.
✉ **Vouliagmenis 22, Neos Kosmos (summer: Poseidonos 3-5, Kalamaki)** ☎ **01 0924 8705** 🚕 **taxi** ⊘ **11pm-late** ⑤ **€7.34/11.74 Fri/Sat**

### Privilege (1, B4)
Consider yourself privileged if you get into this ritzy, pretentious club, popular with the 'in' crowd, although it has more mainstream music and an older crowd than many other clubs. It has recently moved north and the decor turned oriental.
✉ **Sina 7 (cnr Kifissias) Maroussi** ☎ **01 0347 7311**

🚕 **taxi** ⊘ **Wed-Sat 9pm-late** ⑤ **€8.80 Thurs & Sun, €11.74/14.67 Fri/Sat**

### Venue (8, D4)
Resident DJs keep the place buzzing with house, progressive and techno dance tunes in a venue that looks like a set from *Moulin Rouge*. The party atmosphere follows the club to its summer venue.
✉ **Pireos 130 (cnr Alkyoneos), Gazi** ☎ **01 0347 7311** 🚕 **taxi** ⊘ **Thurs-Sat**

*You won't find yourself bored at Lava.*

# LIVE MUSIC

**Café Asante** (7, O10)
It can feel like there's a band in your lounge room in this cosy and casual world-music bar, which hosts regular appearances by eclectic musicians, including the inspirational Armenian Haig Hazdjian. There's a variety of snacks, a lounge area and a great atmosphere (check listings).
✉ **Damareos 78, Pangrati** ☎ **01 0756 0102** 🚌 4 ⏲ **Tues-Sat**

10pm-late Ⓢ min charge €13.21 (inc 1st drink) for a band

**House of Art** (8, B10)
A well-established live music theatre, with changing themes and artists from Greek *laika* and *entekna* to Latin, blues, jazz and even poetry and theatrical performances.
✉ **Sahtouri 4 (cnr Sarri), Psirri**

☎ 01 0321 7678
Ⓜ Monastiraki; Thissio ⏲ performances start 10.30pm
Ⓢ €17.61 (inc 1st drink)

**Half Note Jazz Club** (7, O6) A stylish venue with an international line-up playing classic jazz, folk and occasional Celtic music. It's the original and best venue in Athens for serious jazz. Book a table or you can stand at the bar.
✉ **Trivonianou 17, Mets** ☎ **01 0921 3310** 🚌 2, 11 ⏲ **10.30pm** Ⓢ €23.48/17.61

**Palenque** (6, B10)
A slice of Havana in Athens, there's regular live music, with artists from around the world, salsa parties and flamenco shows. You can take tango lessons earlier in the evenings – and taste the best margaritas in town.
✉ **Farandaton 41, Ambelokipi**
☎ 01 0775 2360
🖥 www.palenque.gr
Ⓜ **Ambelokipi;**
🚌 8, 13 ⏲ **9.30-late**
Ⓢ drinks €8-10

**Rodon Club** (7, D4)
Top-name rock bands, as well as soul and reggae acts perform in this converted movie theatre most Fridays and Saturdays. It's just north of Omonia. Check listings for what's playing.
✉ **Marni 24, Omonia**
☎ 01 0524 7427
🚌 5 ⏲ **from 10pm (for performances)**
Ⓢ varies

## Top Acts Top the Billing

You really have to be in Athens between October and April to see the country's best contemporary artists perform. In summer, most of the top Greek acts go on international tours and work the festival circuit around Greece. In winter, they all return and play in the nightclubs around town.

Most are in modern cabaret-style venues, where you can sit at tables or at the bar, rather than in a stiff concert setting. They are fairly pricey and start very late. It's best to ask around for the best shows in town.

Key venues where you can see popular performers include the converted theatre **Rex,** the modern **Iera Odos** (8, B7; ☎ 01 0342 8272) and **Zygos** (7, L5; Kydathineon 22, Plaka; ☎ 01 0324 1610; €17.61, inc 1st drink) where you can stand at the top-floor bar and watch the show. **Diogenis Studio** (7, A2; Syngrou 259, ☎ 01 0943 5754) is set up like a theatre. The big pop acts are Anna Vissi, Despina Vandi, George Dalaras, Notis Sfakianakis and Ploutarhos. More entekna artists who also give performances include Pyx Lax, Yiannis Kotsiras, Eleftheria Arvanitaki and Alkistis Protopsalti.

Neil Setchfield

*Strumming along: Athens music scene covers all tastes.*

# CLASSICAL MUSIC, OPERA & DANCE

**Athens Concert Hall**
**(6, C7)** An impressive
addition to the Athens
performing arts scene, the
concert hall (Megaron
Moussikis) is considered
one of Europe's most state-
of-the-art cultural centres,
with superb acoustics and
excellent facilities. It presents a rich program of
operas and concerts featuring world-class artists and
performers – both inter-
national and Greek.

It has a music and arts
library, with books, manu-
scripts and musical scores,
plus an exhibition gallery.
✉ **Vasilissis Sofias,
Ambelokipi (program &
tickets also at Omirou
8, Mon-Fri 10am-4pm)**
☎ **01 0728 2333-7**
🖄 **www.megaron.gr**
Ⓜ **Megaro Moussikis**
⑤ depends on perform-
ance; discounts for stu-
dents & under 18s; book
in advance ✗ Allegro
(☎ 01 0728 2150)

**Opera House/
Olympia Theatre**
**(7, G6)** The Greek National
Opera (Ethniki Lyriki Skini)
season runs from November
to June. Performances are
at the Olympia Theatre and
a venue on Ippokratous.
✉ **Akadimias 59**
☎ **01 0360 0180,
01 0361 2461 (box
office)** 🖄 **www
.nationalopera .gr**
Ⓜ **Panepistimio**
⏲ varies ⑤ varies

**Dora Stratou Dance
Theatre (7, M1)**
Performances of traditional
folk dancing by the Dora
Stratou Theatre are a summer tradition on Filopap-
pou Hill. More than 100

*Music at the Megaron is an experience.*

musicians and dancers
perform dances from different regions of Greece in a
colourful 90min show.
Some of the elaborate costumes are museum pieces.
✉ **Filopappou Hill,
Filopappou**

☎ **01 0324 4395, 01
0921 4650 (theatre)**
🖄 **grdance@hol.gr;
users.hol.gr/~grdance**
Ⓜ **Akropoli**
⏲ May-Sept: Tues-Sun
9.30pm
⑤ €14/8

## Festive Athens

Every summer, performances from leading acts in
Greece and around the world take place under the
stars at the ancient Herodes Atticus Theatre. It is one
of the world's most historic venues, with a long tradition of presenting leading classical and contemporary musicians, performers and dance troupes.

Events are held from June-September. For program information and tickets, contact the **Hellenic
Festival box office** (Stadiou 4 (in arcade); ☎ 01
0322 1459; 🖄 www.greekfestival.gr).

The festival also runs the **Epidauros Festival**,
which presents ancient Greek tragedy, comedy and
satire at the ancient Theatre of Epidauros, 2½hrs from
Athens. Set in lush surrounds, the theatre has incred-
ible acoustics, so much so you can hear a pin drop on
the stage from the top rows.

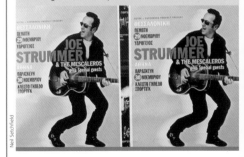

# GREEK MUSIC

The *bouzouki* may be the first thing that comes to mind when you think of Greek music but these days you can hear Greek clubbing music, pop, heavy metal, rap and even hip-hop.

Live performances of traditional *laika* (popular music) are still widespread, as is *rebetika* (the Greek equivalent of the blues) and modern *entekna* (meaning music that is 'artistic' or skillful). Crass pop and dance hits with a disco-*tsifteteli* beat are also popular – and the bouzoukia are still going strong.

Warning: there may be no door charge at many live music places, but the drinks are expensive and there may be a minimum consumption charge.

## Boemissa (6, E6)

A rebetika staple that plays more laika these days, Boemissa is usually lively and raucous, with the dancing moving onto the tables.
✉ Solomou 19, Exarhia ☎ 01 0384 3836 🚕 taxi ⏱ Tues-Sun from 11pm

## Skyladika

The bouzoukia, otherwise known as *skyladika* (doghouses) because of the crooning singers, are an institution, but not everyone's cup of tea. Outrageously expensive, smoky and sleazy, with B-grade performers, they are nonetheless packed out most nights.

If you are game, one of the more established is **Romeo** (7, 04; Kallirrois 4; ☎ 01 0922 4885; summer: Ellinikou 1, Glyfada; ☎ 01 0894 5345). Be warned, it can be outrageously expensive, especially if you sit at a table, with bottles of whisky sold at exorbitant prices.

## Mnisikleous (9, F4)

A classic Plaka taverna, popular for its live music, it has a full-sized stage and dance floor and gets very lively. A good place to come for traditional music and dancing if you can't face a nightclub or rebetadiko.
✉ Mnisikleous 22 (cnr Lyssiou), Plaka ☎ 01 0322 5558 Ⓜ Monastiraki ⏱ 9pm-late

## Mousikes Skies (7, M9)

An intimate venue run by a singer-bouzouki player couple, which presents acoustic laika, entekno and rebetika music and attracts an arty crowd. There's a range of mezedes and an outdoor courtyard in summer.
✉ Athanasias 4, Pangrati ☎ 01 7561 4654 🚕 taxi 🚌 2,4 &11 ⏱ Tues-Sun 11.30pm-late (closed Aug)

## Rebetiki Istoria (7, D10)

One of the older rebetika haunts, it has an authentic grungy, smoky atmosphere with dedicated regulars and a wall of old photos of rebetika musicians. A five-member *compania* sits on a raised platform. It's casual, relaxed,

*Immortal music*

affordable and therefore popular with students.
✉ Ippokratous 181, Exarhia ☎ 01 0642 4937 🚌 2, 11 ⏱ 11.30pm-late

## Stoa Athanaton (7, G4)

Right in the middle of the Athens Central Market, this classic rebetadiko has been around since 1930. It is open day and night and is always lively, with veteran *rebetes* and loyal patrons. There's decent food, too. At the time of research, it was considering opening in summer.
✉ Sofokleous 19 & Stoa Athanaton (arcade), Central Market, Omonia ☎ 01 0321 4362 Ⓜ Omonia ⏱ Mon-Sat 3-7.30pm & 11pm-late

## Taximi (7, E8)

Most of Greece's major rebetika exponents have played here since it opened

20 years ago at the beginning of the rebetika revival. It's gone a little upmarket – and expensive – but it is still a popular and authentic venue. It's best to go weeknights as it gets packed.
✉ cnr Harilaou Trikoupi & Isavron 29, Neapoli ☎ 01 0363 9919, 01 0363 5872
🚖 taxi ⏰ Tues-Sat 11pm-late

## Smashing Plates

Despite the popular perception, there is not much plate-smashing to be had in Greece these days. It's not the done thing in restaurants and in the big cabaret-style bouzoukia clubs the new way of revelling and blowing your euros is to buy trays of carnations and shower your dancing friends or the singers.

At many bars, the party animals also throw paper napkins everywhere when the night heats up. Be warned, these acts of merrymaking can be very pricey.

# CINEMAS

One of the delights of summer is watching movies under the moonlight. The outdoor cinemas that hung on throughout the threat from video, air-conditioning and multiplexes are enjoying a revival. Unlike most European countries, the Greeks don't dub English-language films, so don't miss the experience. To check movie listings, see the English edition of *Kathimerini* (inside the *International Herald Tribune*) or the *Athens News*.

## OUTDOOR

**Cine Pari (7, L5)**
A traditional old rooftop cinema in Plaka with great views of the Acropolis and stereo sound.
✉ Kydathineon 22, Plaka ☎ 01 0322 2071
Ⓜ Syntagma ⏰ May-Oct, check listings
⑤ €5.87 ♿

**Aigli (7, L7)**
The oldest outdoor cinema (it used to play silent movies) re-opened in 2000 in the Zappeio Gardens. It has a deal with the restaurant next door for wine and gourmet snack packs during the film or a dinner and movie package.
✉ Zappeio Gardens, Zappeio ☎ 01 0336 9369 🚌 2, 11, 14
⏰ check listings
⑤ €6.46 ♿

**Afroditi (8, D3)**
A modern theatre in this semi-industrial area, with a big screen and lounge chairs in the first row. There's a nice bar and you can sit at a table and eat a buffet dinner as you watch a film.
✉ Andronikou 7-9, Rouf ☎ 01 0342 5890

🚖 taxi ⏰ check listings ⑤ €5.57 ♿

**Dexameni (6, D3)**
Halfway up to Lykavittos Hill, Dexameni has been spruced up, with deck chairs, two bars, Dolby SR, table seating and a gorgeous wall of bougainvillea.
✉ Plateia Dexameni, Kolonaki ☎ 01 0360 2363 Ⓜ Evangelismos
⏰ check listings
⑤ €6.46/4.69 ♿

**Thisseion (7, L2)**
Across from the Acropolis, near the bustling cafes of Iraklidon, this is a lovely old-style cinema with a snack bar and garden setting. Sit towards the back if you want to catch a glimpse of the glowing edifice.
✉ Apostolou Pavlou 7, Thisio ☎ 01 0342 0864
🚋 Thissio ⏰ check listings ⑤ €5.87 ♿

## Premiere Nights

Launched in 1995, the annual Athens Film Festival, Premiere Nights (☎ 01 0606 1413, e www.aiff.gr), screens an eclectic selection of international and Greek independent cinema.

Held in September at the refurbished Attikon and Apollon Renault cinemas, it is organised by leading movie magazine *Cinema*, in conjunction with the Municipality of Athens.

*Movies by moonlight at the Thisseion.*

## INDOOR

### Apollon & Attikon Renault (7, H5)

This historic 1960s theatre has been beautifully renovated with the latest screen-and-sound technology. There's a great refreshments bar and comfortable seating. The cinema hosts the annual Athens Film Festival.

⌧ Stadiou 19, Syntagma ☎ 01 0323 6811, 01 0322 8821 Ⓜ Panepistimiou; Syntagma ◷ check listings ⓢ €5.87 ⚱

### Asty (7, H6)

A favourite for avant-garde moviegoers, this old theatre has plenty of character and an eclectic selection of arthouse movies.

⌧ Korai 4, Syntagma ☎ 01 0322 1925 Ⓜ Panepistimiou ◷ check listings ⓢ €5.28 ⚱

### Athinais I & II

(8, A4) There are two cinemas in this modern, multipurpose venue in a renovated old silk factory, which also has a restaurant, brasserie, cafe, gallery and gift store.

⌧ Kastorias 34-36, Votanikos, Gazi ☎ 01 0348 0000 🚖 taxi ◷ check listings ⓢ €5.87/4.99 ⚱

### Petit Palai-Filmcentre 2000 (7, L10)

Don't be fooled by the modern foyer in what looks like a normal apartment block. In the basement is a quirky flashback cinema with balcony and old-style bar. It's part of the Filmcentre 2000 network that screens arthouse films.

⌧ cnr Rizari & Hironos, Pangrati ☎ 01 0729 1800, 01 0724 3707 Ⓜ Evangelismos ◷ check listings ⓢ €5.87/4.98 ⚱

### Village Park Renti

(1, D2) This rather incongruous 20-cinema entertainment complex in Athens' western suburbs has dramatically increased cinema admissions since it opened in 1999. Run by the Australian cinema chain, it has love seats, air-conditioning, shops, eateries and lots of open space – including parking for 1800 cars.

⌧ Thivon & Petrou Ralli, Renti ☎ 01 0427 8600 🚌 21 from Pireos 🚌 A18, B18 (from Menandrou) ◷ check listings ⓢ €6.75 ⚱

## Parnitha Casino

It isn't one of the world's most glamorous casinos (1, A2; ☎ 01 0246 9111; Parnitha) but the location in the Mt Parnitha National Park, 40km outside Athens, makes for a pleasant trip. Access is by cable car, and the surrounding natural landscape is a welcome break from the concrete sprawl.

The huge number of international consortia bidding for a stake in the run-down, soon-to-be privatised facility seem confident they can turn the complex into a major 24hr gambling complex of international standing.

A €7.3 million refurbishment of the casino and the two hotels is underway, and 200 slot machines and new gaming tables have been installed.

# GAY & LESBIAN ATHENS

The gay scene seems to be gaining momentum and prominence in Athens, with several clubs operating around town, concentrated mostly in the Kolonaki and Makrigianni areas. Most bars have a €5-8 door charge, which includes your first drink.

### Alekos' Island (6, D3)
One of the first gay bars in Athens, run by an artist whose works adorn the walls. The candlelit lounge-style hangout has a homey feel – Alekos even bakes the cakes at the bar. Attracts an older crowd and last year hosted the Athens bears meeting.
✉ **Tsakalof 42, Kolonaki** ☎ **01 0723 9163 Ⓜ Syntagma**
🕓 6pm-late

### Athens Relax (7, E4)
A men-only private *hammam* (steam bath) and bar in a seedy part of Omonia. No inside info on this one, I'm afraid.
✉ **Xouthou 8, Omonia** ☎ **01 0522 2866 Ⓜ Omonia**
🕓 Mon-Sat 1-8.30pm
Ⓢ steam bath €13.21

### Bee (9, B2)
The food here is excellent, but Bee has increasingly become more of a gay and lesbian hang-out. The bar opens directly onto the street, where the hip young crowd spills out on most nights. Very arty decor and a regularly changing, innovative window display.
✉ **Miaouli & Themidos, Psirri** ☎ **01 0321 2624** 🚇 **Monastiraki**
🕓 8pm-1.30am, Sat & Sun lunch from noon

### The Guys (7, N5)
A cosy little bar on the east side of Syngrou, ideal for a quiet drink. Cool music and an island bar, the walls are covered with pictures of movie stars.
✉ **Lembesi 10, Makrigianni** ☎ **01 0921 4244 Ⓜ Akropoli**
🕓 11pm-late (closed Tues)

### Kirkis (8, E9)
A popular gay and lesbian cafe-bar, under the Lizard bar. It is a casual meeting point before heading off to the clubs. There's a good range of meze for lunch and dinner.
✉ **Apostolou Pavlou 31, Thisio** ☎ **01 0346 6960** 🚇 **Thissio**
🕓 10am-3am

### Lamda (7, N5)
After 2am, this three-level club is one of the busiest gay clubs in Athens, attracting a diverse crowd, including some women. There is a tropical aquarium behind the dance floor, a bar and a DJ playing mainstream and Greek club music. There are videos and two back rooms in the basement.
✉ **Lembesi 15 (cnr Syngrou), Makrigianni** ☎ **01 0942 4202 Ⓜ Akropoli** 🕓 **closed Aug**

### Lizard (8, E9)
This popular gay *steki* (hang-out) upstairs from Kirkis is the place to start on Sunday night. With Acropolis views while you dance and a (relatively) quiet lounge area at the back, it's a casual bar with diverse music and a young, friendly crowd. Greek music goes till late.
✉ **Apostolou Pavlou 31, Thisio** ☎ **01 0346 8670** 🚇 **Thissio**
🕓 Fri-Sun 11pm-late

### Sodade (8, A5)
Worth a trip to the former industrial zone near the old gasworks, where the industrial theme continues inside this funky venue. Sodade attracts a mixed lesbian and gay crowd and has the latest dance music and a huge video screen out the back. There are comfy cushions in the long candlelit courtyard outside.
✉ **Triptolemou 10, Gazi** ☎ **01 0346 8657** 🌐 **www.sodade.gr** 🚕 **taxi** 🕓 11pm-late

## Gay Beaches
The most popular beach for gays is **Limanakia**, at the rocky coves of Varkiza, which is part-nudist (as in parts of the beach).

Take the A2 Glyfada bus (summer: express E2) in front of the Athens Academy on Panepistimiou (change at Glyfada, take 115 or 116 to Limanakia B stop).

# SPECTATOR SPORTS

Most of the major sporting venues in Athens are being upgraded in time for the Olympics and will be closed for large parts of 2002 to 2004. Several clubs will be moved around between venues.

After 2004, the city will be left with world-class sports stadiums. Visitors wanting to catch some sport in the interim are advised to contact the clubs or sporting bodies direct for venue and match information or check the English-language press.

The Greek Secretariat for Sport has a website ( **e** www.sport.gov.gr) with information on all sports organisations and stadiums.

## Soccer

Soccer is the most popular sport in Greece, which fields two teams in the European's Champions league. The top three teams in Greece are Panathinaikos, AEK and Olympiakos.

Information on all Greek first division clubs, including games fixtures, can be found on **e** www.onefootball.com. Generally, tickets to major games can be bought on the day at the venue itself. Big football games take place at the Olympic Stadium in Maroussi, although this venue was to close for some time before 2004.

## Basketball

Greeks are also keen basketball fans and the biggest games take place at the Stadium of Peace and Friendship (1, D2; ☎ 01 0489 3000; Ethnarhou Makariou) in Palio Faliro. Greek basketball is dominated by Piraeus-based Olympiakos, which did well in the European championships in the early 90s. Greece fields six teams in the Euro League.

## Athletics

For athletics fans, the annual Tsiklitiria Athens Grand Prix takes place in the summer. This is where Maurice Green broke the world record in 1999. Tickets and information are available at **e** www.tsiklitiria.org.

## Horse Racing

The Faliro Ippodromo (1, D3; ☎ 01 09417 761; D' Faliron) race track holds races every Monday, Wednesday and Friday at 3pm.

*Sports fans may get a bit shirty waiting for the Olympics.*

# places to stay

**A**thens' accommodation industry is undergoing a major shake-up, with new hotels being built and many older hotels being upgraded and spruced up to house the thousands of visitors expected for the Olympics in 2004.

More than 10,000 new beds are expected to be created and the overall quality of accommodation improved, although presumably prices will rise accordingly.

That said, there are many fine, established hotels for business and leisure travellers, from grand former palaces to contemporary international hotels and smaller family-run affairs. Overall, the industry is becoming more professional and customer-oriented. And many hotels are investing in soundproof glass.

Neil Setchfield

## Room Rates

The categories listed here indicate the cost per night of a standard double room, based on the median of the official price ranges. Hotels have also been judged on location and proximity to the centre and main tourist attractions.

| | |
|---|---|
| Deluxe | from €325 |
| Top End | €220-324 |
| Mid-Range | €105-219 |
| Budget | under €105 |

## Before you Dial

Greece is in the process of entirely changing its phone numbering system – of course it is being done in a couple of stages just to make it confusing. So before you pick up the phone to make that reservation, check out the telephone information on p. 116.

The phone numbers listed in this book are valid until October 2002.

Greece's hotel rating system is also in the process of changing to the five-star international system. This long-awaited change will bring hotel classifications into line with accepted standards for rooms and services. Many of Athens' existing hotels have the top rating and price, but can be very disappointing compared with international standards.

The current classification system is controlled by the Greek National Tourist Organisation (GNTO, or EOT in Greek), which obligates hotels to post official rates on the back of the hotel room door. The official prices are often much more expensive compared with what you will pay if you haggle or book through an agency (especially during off-peak periods).

The official EOT categories are: L for Luxury and A, B, C, D, E for 1st to 5th class. Staff in the first few categories are expected to speak several languages.

As prices can vary greatly according to season and availability, check with hotels for special rates – and haggle – as the official rates are definitely at the higher end.

Neil Setchfield

*Looking for NJV Athens Plaza?*

# DELUXE

## Sofitel Athens Airport

This brand-spanking new hotel (☎ 01 0354 4000; fax 01 0354 4444; e h3167@accorhotels .com; www.sofitel.com) opened next to the new Athens airport in November 2001. It is the only hotel near the airport and is also 12km from the port of Rafina, which services Mykonos and the Cyclades. The eight-storey hotel has all the expected facilities for a transit hotel including executive suites, a business centre, conference facilities, gym, health club and indoor pool.

### Andromeda (6, B8)
A member of the Small Luxury Hotels of the World, this boutique hotel is in a quiet, tree-lined street behind the Athens Concert Hall and the US embassy. Stylish and intimate, it has all the mod cons on a smaller scale, with 12 executive apartments across the street.
✉ Timoleontos Vassou 22, Ambelokipi ☎ 01 0641 5000; fax 01 0646 6361 e reservations@ andromedaathens.gr; www.andromedaa thens.gr ⓂAmbelokipi ✕ Etrusco

### Astir Palace (1, E4)
A luxury seaside resort on a peninsula south of Athens, this three-hotel complex is a super-exclusive place to enjoy the sea and sunshine. Moneyed Athenians often come here to escape the city for weekends in the summer. A shuttle bus commutes to the centre daily, but it is a hike into town.
✉ Apollonos 40, Lemos Vouliagmenis ☎ 01 0890 2000; fax 01 0896 2582 e aspa-res@astir.gr; http://www.astir.gr 🚖 taxi ✕ Club House

### Athens Hilton (6, E6)
Extensive renovations will no doubt restore the Hilton to its former status as one of the best Athens hotels, but it is closed until early 2003.
✉ Vasilissis Sofias 46, Ilissia ☎ 01 0728 1000; fax 01 0728 1111 e fom.athens@hilton .com Ⓜ Evangelismos ✕ Byzantino

Hilton on hiatus

### Athenaeum Inter-Continental
(7, P2) An ultra-modern, international-standard hotel with impeccable service, spacious rooms and a marble lobby boasting some serious art. There are Acropolis views from some rooms, a health club, big pool and VIP club. A little out of the centre, it's good for business travellers – and there's a great seafood buffet on the rooftop restaurant.
✉ Syngrou 89-93, Neos Kosmos ☎ 01 0920 6000; fax 01 0924 3000 e athens@interconti .com; www.interconti .com 🚖 taxi ✕ Premiere ⚥

### Divani Caravel
(6, E6) Renovated in 1999, with the latest facilities, soundproof windows and a marble lobby, the Caravel is close to the National Gallery and only a short walk from many museums. It has a good reputation for service, hosts many conferences and has an outdoor pool (heated and covered in winter), roof garden and fitness centre.
✉ Vassileos Alexandrou 2, Ilissia ☎ 01 0720 7000; fax 01 0723 6683 e divanis@divani caravel.gr; www .divanicaravel.gr Ⓜ Evangelismos ✕ Millennium ⚥

### Grand Bretagne
(9, C10) This Athens landmark and former palace is definitely grand, with a history, prestige and location that make this one of the most exclusive hotels in the city. It will be closed for 2002 while it undergoes a major upgrade.
✉ Vassileos Georgiou A. 1, Syntagma Sq ☎ 01 0333 0000; fax 01 0322 8034 e gbhotel@otenet.gr Ⓜ Syntagma ✕ GB Corner ⚥

### The Margi Hotel
(2, C7) Renovated in 2000, this impressive boutique hotel is right next to the beach, but you may not want to leave the cabana

Neil Setchfield

pool which is stylishly decked out in teak and rattan furniture. Many rooms have sea views and the facilities are excellent, including access for the mobility impaired. A great option in summer if you don't need to be in town.

✉ **Litous 11, Vouliagmeni** ☎ **01 0896 2061; fax 01 0896 0229** e **themargi@ themargi.gr; www.the margi.gr** 🚖 **taxi** ✗ **Café Tabac** ♿

### NJV Athens Plaza

**(9, C9)** A more contemporary alternative on Syntagma Square, this hotel was recently renovated by the Grecotel hotel group, with Italian designer decor and individually decorated suites. It's central and comfortable. A family plan allows children under 12 to stay with their parents free.

✉ **Vassileos Georgiou A. 2, Syntagma Sq** ☎ **01 0325 5301-9; fax 01 0323 5856** e **ath.plaza@ath .forthnet.gr; www .grandotel.gr** Ⓜ **Syntagma** ✗ **Parliament** ♿

### Pentelikon (3, A5)

One of the most decadent options in Athens, the luxury Pentelikon is in a neoclassical mansion, with swimming pool, manicured garden and beautifully furnished rooms. Faultless service and a Michelin-rated restaurant make it a real treat.

✉ **Diligianni 66, Kefalari** ☎ **01 0623 0650-7; fax 01 0801 0314**

*Service with a smile.*

e **pentelikon@ otenet.gr; www.hotel pentelikon.gr** 🚖 **taxi** ✗ **Vardis (p. 87)**

## TOP END

### Alexandros (6, B8)

A small luxury hotel renovated in 1999, the Alexandros is popular with executives and business travellers. It has all the latest facilities, including a conference centre and business services, as well as a pleasant environment with a contemporary colour scheme combining natural timbers, exposed brickwork and marble. The upper floors have generous balconies with views over the city.

✉ **Timoleontos Vassou 8, Plateia Mavili, Ambelokipi** ☎ **01 0643 0464; fax 01 0644 1084** e **airotel@otenet.gr; www.airotel-hotels .com** Ⓜ **Megaro Moussikis** ✗ **Don Giovanni**

### Athens Holiday Inn

**(6, E7)** Popular with executives, the hotel was extensively renovated in 1998 to cater for business travellers and tourists, with voice mail and all the expected in-room features. The rooms are light and modern and the rooftop health club has the latest in equipment and a pool.

✉ **Mihalokopoulou 50, Ilissia** ☎ **01 0727 8000; fax 01 0727 8600** e **holinn@ath.forthnet .gr; www.hiathens greece.com** Ⓜ **Megaro Moussikis**

### Divani Palace Acropolis (7, N4)

This stylish hotel is very close to Plaka and, as the name suggests, the Acropolis. It has a business centre and both an indoor and outdoor pool. Ancient ruins found in the foundation have been incorporated into the hotel's design.

✉ **Parthenonos 19-25, Makrigianni** ☎ **01 0928 0100; fax 01 0921 4993** e **divanis@ divaniacropolis.gr; www.divaniacropolis.gr** Ⓜ **Akropoli**

### Kefalari Suites (3, B5)

A hotel in a stylish building in the heart of Kifissia, Kefalari has themed rooms (from French chateau to African Queen) all with kitchenettes. It's not in town, but there are plenty of good restaurants nearby.

✉ **Pentelis 1 (cnr Kolokotroni), Kifissia** ☎ **01 0623 3333; fax 01 0623 3330** e **info @kefalarisuites.gr; www.kefalarisuites.gr** 🚖 **taxi** ✗ **Klik Cafe** ♿

Neil Setchfield

**Ledra Marriott** (7, P2)
An Athenian classic favoured by many international stars, this hotel has been revamped, with a new health club and has a pool with great views of the Acropolis. There is a shuttle bus into town, excellent service and facilities and an impressive 1000-plus piece chandelier in the lounge.
✉ Syngrou 113-115, Neos Kosmos ☎ 01 0930 0000; fax 01 0935 8603 ⓔ marriott@ otenet.gr; www .marriott.com 🚌 040 from Syntagma ✗ Kona Kai ♿

**Metropolitan** (7, P2)
A major refurbishment has made this one of the more contemporary hotels in Athens, with excellent business and conference facilities and efficient service. Its location is the biggest drawback, with nothing interesting within walking distance, although it is close to the port of Piraeus and has an outdoor pool

and roof garden.
✉ Syngrou 385, Palio Faliro ☎ 01 0947 1000; fax 01 0947 1010 ⓔ metropolitan@ chandris.gr; www .chandris.gr 🚖 taxi ✗ Trocadero

**Omonia Grand** (7, F4)
Reputedly the capital's funkiest hotel, the refurbished Grand is certainly trying to attract a more hip clientele to the Omonia area, which is undergoing its own major facelift. Apart from the out-there pop art foyer, it has business facilities, well-appointed rooms and a creative restaurant menu.
✉ Pireos 2, Omonia ☎ 01 0523 5230; fax 01 0523 6341 ⓔ www .grandotel.gr Ⓜ Omonia ✗ Omonia Times

**Park Hotel** (7, C6)
Opposite the Pedion Areos Park, the Park is off the main hotel drag, but is a good if nondescript city hotel, with comfortable rooms and business facilities and in-house hair and beauty services.
✉ Alexandras 10, Areos Park ☎ 01 0883 2711-9; fax 01 0823 8420 ⓔ park-hotel @otenet.gr; www .park-hotel.gr 🚇 Victoria ✗ Alexandra's

**St George Lycabettus** (6, D3) This is a delightful historic hotel on the slopes of Lykavittos Hill, with great views of the city and an impressive art collection. Rooms are modern, stylish and well appointed, and the lavish suites have accommodated royalty. There's a rooftop pool and bar and two restaurants. The uphill hike is the only catch.
✉ Kleomenous 2, Plateia Dexameni, Kolonaki ☎ 01 0729 0711-9; fax 01 0724 7610 ⓔ info@ sglycabettus.gr; www.sglycabettus.gr Ⓜ Evangelismos ✗ Le Grand Balcon

**Theoxenia Palace** (3, B5) Old-world elegance and modern-city comforts come in a fine location, opposite Kefalari Park in Kifissia. The hotel has stylish and light rooms, conference facilities, and a state-of-the-art gym that looks out onto the outdoor pool.
✉ Filadelfeos 2 (cnr Kolokotroni), Kefalari ☎ 01 0623 3622-6; fax 01 0623 1675 ⓔ theoxeniapalace @attglobal.net; www.theoxeniapalace .com 🚖 taxi ✗ Click Cafe ♿

## Children & Pets
Most top hotels can provide babysitting services if given prior notice. Make the request when booking or at least a day before you need one. Hotels offering this service have special arrangements with registered childcare providers. Rates range from €5.87-21.50 per hr and increase after midnight (including paying for a taxi if it's late). A surprising number of Athens' hotels will accommodate pets (with prior notice). Check with individual hotels.

# MID-RANGE

### Amalia (9, F10)
Opposite the National Gardens, and near Plaka, the Amalia has good facilities as well as a roof garden, making it great value for the price.
✉ Amalias 10, Syntagma ☎ 01 0323 7301-9; fax 01 0323 8792 📧 hotamal@ hellasnet.gr; www .amalia.gr Ⓜ Syntagma ✗ Aigli (p. 84)

### Dorian Inn (7, F3)
The Dorian is a central, standard hotel on busy Pireos with clean, comfortable rooms and suites, a restaurant and bar, as well as a rooftop pool with views of the Acropolis and Lykavittos.
✉ Pireos 15-17, Omonia ☎ 01 0523 9782; fax 01 0522 6196 📧 doarianh@otenet.gr; www.greekhotel.com/ athens/dorianinn Ⓜ Omonia ✗ Athinaikon

### Electra Palace (9, F7)
Close to Plaka, the dated Electra Palace was being extensively renovated and was due to open anew in May 2002. Some have balconies overlooking the Acropolis with tables for you to eat breakfast or have a drink at, but the best views are from the roof garden bar and pool.
✉ Navarhou Nikodimou 18, Plaka ☎ 01 0337 0000, 01 0324 1401; fax 01 0324 1875 📧 electra hotels@ath.forthnet.gr Ⓜ Syntagma ✗ Daphne's (p. 80)

### Esperia Palace (9, A8)
It's not much to look at from the street, but the Esperia has been tastefully renovated inside, with good facilities. It's in a handy location, just a short walk from Syntagma.
✉ Stadiou 22, Panepistimiou ☎ 01 0323 8001-9; fax 01 0323 8100 📧 www.esperia.gr Ⓜ Panepistimiou; Syntagma ✗ Palia Vouli

*Esperia Palace*

### Herodion (7, M4)
Good service and comfortable, modern rooms make this a pleasant place to stay, right near the Herodes Atticus Theatre (after which it is named). There's a rooftop terrace with Parthenon views and a shady courtyard.
✉ Rovertou Galli 4, Makrigianni ☎ 01 0923 6832-6; fax 01 0923 5857 📧 herodion@otenet.gr Ⓜ Akropoli ✗ Strofi (p. 75) ⚕

### Novotel Athenes (7, D3)
Omonia is gradually undergoing a beautification and desleazing, but has some way to go before the area loses its grittiness. The location does not seem to affect the high occupancy rate of this modern hotel, which has good facilities and city and Acropolis views from the rooftop pool and bar area.
✉ Michail Voda 4-6, Plateia Vathis, Omonia ☎ 01 0820 0700-1; fax 01 0820 0777 📧 novotel @hol.gr Ⓜ Larissis

### Parthenon (7, M5)
Located at the foot of the Acropolis, close to Plaka, this hotel is geared towards the business traveller, but makes an ideal base for checking out the sites. It has comfortable, clean rooms, many with balconies and views.
✉ Makri 6, Makrigianni ☎ 01 0923 4594-8; fax 01 0923 5797 📧 airotel @netplan.gr Ⓜ Akropoli ⚕

### Titania (7, F5)
The 400-room Titania was renovated in 1998. It is a comfortable, modern central hotel with large rooms and good facilities for the price. There are great views over the city at night from the rooftop piano bar and the restaurant is well recommended.
✉ Panepistimiouu 52, Omonia ☎ 01 0330 0111; fax 01 0330 7000 📧 titania@titania.gr; www.titania.gr Ⓜ Omonia; Panepistimiou ✗ The Olive Garden (p. 82) ⚕

Neil Setchfield

# BUDGET

### Achilleas (9, C7)
Modern and simple, this small, centrally located hotel is in a side street off busy Syntagma. With all the basics, including mini-bar, air-conditioning and TV, it offers good value for money.
✉ Lekka 21, Syntagma
☎ 01 0323 3197; fax 01 0322 2412
📧 achilleas@ tourhotel.gr
Ⓜ Syntagma

### Acropolis House
(9, F7) A grand old pension in a 19th-century Plaka residence favoured by artists and academics, this hotel has 20 large but basic rooms with original frescoes, clean, simple decor and friendly owners. Some rooms have their own bathrooms just outside in the hallway, but not all have air-conditioning.
✉ Kodrou 6-8, Plaka
☎ 01 0322 2344; fax 01 0324 4143
Ⓜ Syntagma

### Acropolis View (7, M3)
There are indeed views of the Acropolis from many of the rooms, although the best views are from the roof terrace. Other rooms look over Filopappou Hill. This is a quiet, basic place to stay near the Herodes Atticus Theatre.
✉ Webster 10 (off Rovertou Galli), Makrigianni ☎ 01 0921 7303; fax 01 0923 0705 Ⓜ Akropoli

### Athenian Inn (6, D4)
A small but distinguished place in the heart of posh Kolonaki, this was a favourite of writer Lawrence

*Cool your heels at the Achilleas.*

Durrell and is often full of visiting archaeologists. The comfortable, unpretentious rooms have air-conditioning, but some can be a bit drab and cramped.
✉ Haritos 22, Kolonaki
☎ 01 0723 8097; fax 01 0724 2268
Ⓜ Evangelismos
✕ Azul (p. 78)

### Castella (5, C8)
A small, good-value, renovated hotel overlooking Piraeus' picturesque Mikrolimano harbour, Castella has modern decor and facilities, including a rooftop bar with garden. The busy promenade below is full of restaurants and bars, but the hotel is high enough to avoid the noise.
✉ Vasileos Pavlou 75, Kastella ☎ 01 0411 4735-7; fax 01 0417 5716 🚕 taxi ✕ Jimmy & the Fish (p. 86)

### Hermes Hotel (9, E7)
This is an inviting hotel with impeccably clean, air-conditioned rooms in a central location. It is very reasonably priced and great value for the city centre.

The manager runs a helpful travel agency in the lobby.
✉ Apollonos 19, Plaka
☎ 01 0323 5514, fax 01 0323 2073 Ⓜ Syntagma
✕ Furin Kazan (p. 84)

### Hotel Cecil (9, A3)
This fine, old, family-run hotel was recently renovated, making it a pleasant and good-value place to stay. It has polished timber floors, high moulded ceilings and 36 tastefully furnished rooms with TV and minibar.
✉ Athinas 39, Monastiraki ☎ 01 0321 7079; fax 01 0321 8005 📧 cecil@ netsmart.gr; www .cecil-hotel.com
🚇 Monastiraki

### Hotel Cypria (9, C7)
A small hotel in the heart of town, the Cypria changed names and management in 1999. It offers excellent value, comfort and convenience just off the Ermou shopping precinct. Rooms have a minibar and room service.
✉ Diomeias 5, Syntagma ☎ 01 0323 8034-8; fax 01 0324 8792 📧 diomeia@hol.gr
Ⓜ Syntagma

### President (6, A9)
Modern and clean, the President is value for money given the facilities, although it is just outside the city centre. It has an outdoor pool and roof garden.
✉ Kifissias 43, Ambelokipi ☎ 01 0698 9000; fax 01 0692 4968
📧 president @president.gr; www.president.gr
Ⓜ Ambelokipi ♿

# facts for the visitor

Neil Setchfield

*The ancient Parthenon refers to the worship of Athena, the patroness of Athens.*

# ARRIVAL & DEPARTURE

Athens is a busy European hub, well serviced by direct flights from most parts of the world, including the USA, Australia and Asia. It can also be accessed by ship from Italy, via the city of Patras, by ferries from Turkey and Cyprus, and by train through the Balkans and Turkey.

## Air

The new Eleftherios Venizelos international airport near Spata, 27km north-east of Athens, opened in March 2001. Situated among the vineyards and olive groves of east Attica, it is named after the country's leading 20th-century politician. Facilities are radically better than those at the former airport in Ellnikon (which will be redeveloped), although some bemoan its lack of character.

One of the most hi-tech European airports, it has state-of-the-art baggage security systems as well as cafes, shops and banks. The airport is connected to the city and the ports of Piraeus and Rafina via express buses and the metro (a direct rail link is expected by 2004). It is also equipped to deal with special-needs travellers, with lifts for the mobility impaired and even toilets with Braille.

### Left Luggage

Pacific Baggage Storage near Exit 1 in the Arrivals Terminal (☎ 01 0353 0160) charges €2.93 per day (small), €4.10 (medium) and €5.28 (large) for the first 10 days. Rates halve for every day after that.

### Information

General Inquiries
   ☎ 01 0357 1037, 01 0357 1065 or 01 0353 0000

Flight Information
   ☎ 01 0353 0000 (all airlines)

Hotel Booking Service
   ☎ 01 03530 445-7
   (GNTO Airport Office)

Airport Information Online
   **e** www.aia.gr

### Airport Access

**Train** The suburban rail extension, due to finish in 2004, will cut travel time considerably. At the time of writing, the quickest way to the airport was a combination of train and bus. Take the metro to Ethniki Amina and catch the E94 express airport bus. The trip takes 25-35mins.

**Bus** The E95 airport express bus (24hrs) leaves from Amalias Ave (opposite Othonos) in Syntagma, outside the Parliament, every 10mins during peak times, and takes about an hour – longer when traffic is bad. Bus E96 connects the airport with Piraeus and leaves from Plateia Karaïskaki in Piraeus.

Although buses run 24hrs, the metro stops just after midnight. A one-day travel ticket (€2.93), which gets you to or from the airport and is valid for 24hrs on all transport, can be purchased from the airport bus kiosk, metro terminals and transport kiosks around Athens.

**Taxi** Cabs can take longer than public transport if traffic congestion is bad. Expect to pay between €14.67 and €17.60 to or from the city centre, which includes freeway toll and baggage surcharge. Remember, tariffs to the airport are single and not double (unless travel time coincides with tariff changes (see p.111).

## Bus

International coaches from Turkey, Bulgaria and Albania arrive at Stathmos Peloponnesou, next to the Larisis railway station (☎ 01 0529 8740).

## Train

Greece is part of the Eurail network. Inter-Rail or Global passes can only be bought by residents of non-European countries before arriving in Europe.

International trains arrive at Larisis station, as do trains from Thessaloniki and the Peloponnese. For ticketing and schedules information call ☎ 01 0529 7777 or get online at e www.ose.gr.

The Greek Railroad Organisation (OSE) has offices at Sina 6, Syntagma (☎ 01 0362 4402-6) and Karolou 1, Omonia (☎ 01 0524 0647).

## Sea

Piraeus is the busiest port in Greece with a bewildering number of departures and destinations, including daily services to the islands (except the Ionians and the Sporades). Ferries from Italy dock at Patras in the Peloponnese, and Igoumenitsa in north-western Greece.

## Travel Documents

### Passport

You need a valid passport to enter Greece (or ID card for European Union (EU) nationals), which must also be produced when registering in a hotel or pension.

### Visa

No visa is required for stays of less than 90 days for nationals from Australia, Canada, EU countries, USA, Israel, Japan, New Zealand, Norway, Switzerland and most South American countries. Others, and those wanting longer stays, should check with their local Greek embassy.

## Customs

There are no longer duty-free restrictions within the EU, but random customs searches are still made for drugs. Customs inspections for non-EU tourists are usually cursory, although there are spot checks.

You can bring an unlimited amount of foreign currency and travellers cheques into the country but if you intend to leave with more than US$1000 in cash you must declare the sum upon entry.

Import regulations for medicines are strict. Importing Codeine-based medication is illegal without a doctor's certificate. Dogs and cats must have a vet's certificate.

Exporting antiquities (anything over 100 years old) is strictly forbidden without an export permit. It is an offence to remove even the smallest article from an archaeological site.

## Duty Free

There are no duty-free sales within the EU. Non-EU residents can bring 200 cigarettes or 50 cigars; 1L of spirits or 2L of wine; 50g of perfume; 250mL of eau de Cologne and gifts with a value of up to €150. Cameras, laptops and videos should be declared and a stamp put in your passport, otherwise you may be asked for proof that you did not buy them in Greece.

## Departure Tax

Airport tax for domestic flights is €21.17. For international flights to EU countries the tax is €23.59 or €33.59 for other destinations. Both taxes are pre-paid with your ticket.

# GETTING AROUND

The sparkling new metro system has made getting around the centre of Athens relatively painless, and with the extension of the whole network it should ease the city's notorious traffic congestion. Athens also has an extensive bus and trolley (electric cable bus) network.

## Travel Passes

Daily travel passes (€2.93) for buses, trolleys and the metro (including travel to and from the airport) are valid for 24hrs.

## Bus

Since most of the major sights in Athens are within walking distance of the centre, chances are you won't need public transport.

Suburban Buses (blue & white) operate every 15mins, from 5am-midnight. Timetables can be obtained from the GNTO, its website (e www .gnto.gr) or the Athens Urban Transport Organisation (OASA) website (e www.oasa.gr).

Bus travel in Greece is inexpensive, usually comfortable and relatively fast. For information on routes, schedules and tickets call ☎ 185.

Terminal A, north-west of Omonia Square (Kifissou 100; ☎ 01 0513 4588, 01 0512 4910), has buses to the Peloponnese, Ionian islands and western Greece. The only public transport to the centre is bus 051 to Omonia. The service stops midnight-5am.

Terminal B, is 5km north of Omonia off Liossion (Ag. Dimitriou Oplon; ☎ 01 0831 7096).

There are buses for most Attica destinations leaving from the Mavromateon terminal (cnr Alexandras & 28 Oktovriou-Patission; ☎ 01 0821 3203). Buses to Rafina and Marathon leave from stops 150m north on Mavromateon.

## Train

The new metro's coverage is still largely confined to the centre. The stations have impressive displays of antiquities and public art, which make Syntagma and Evangelismos virtually museums in their own right. Trains run 5am-midnight, every 3mins during peak periods, then every 10mins.

Three lines make up the network: the old Kifissia-Piraeus ISAP-Line 1 (green line), Line 2 (red line) from Sepolia to Dafni and Line 3 (blue line) to Ethniki Amina. There are transfer stations at Attiki, Omonia (Line 1 & 2) and Syntagma (Line 3 only).

Ticket pricing is complicated. Travel on Lines 2 and 3 costs €0.73, while Line 1 is split into three sections across: Piraeus-Monastiraki, Monastiraki-Attiki and Attiki-Kifissia (€0.58 one section, €0.73 for two or more). Tickets must be validated at the machines on platform entrances. Tickets are valid for 90mins and allow connections with trains going in one direction, but you cannot leave and re-enter the station using the same ticket.

## Boat

### Ferry

Weekly ferry schedules, company details and tickets are available from tourist offices, online (e www .greekferries.gr) and in the English edition *Kathimerini* of the *International Herald Tribune*. The main companies are Minoan Lines (☎ 01 0408 0006-16, e www.ferries.gr/minoan) with their Superfast Ferries, and Blue Star Ferries (☎ 01 0322 6400, e www.bluestar.com).

To book a cabin or take a car on board, it is advisable to buy a ticket in advance. Otherwise, there are agents selling tickets in Piraeus (especially around Plateia Karaï-skaki). You can also buy tickets on the ferry. Most ferries to the Cycladic, Saronic and Dodecanese islands and Crete leave from Piraeus or Rafina.

### Hydrofoils/Dolphins

Hydrofoil services operate from the main port in Piraeus or Marina Zea and cut travel time by almost half, making them a very convenient way to get to islands. However, strong wind conditions can lead to cancellations. Hellas Flying Dolphins (☎ 01 0419 9000; Mon-Fri 8am-8pm, Sat & Sun 8am-4pm) has regular services and takes credit card bookings. For information and schedules see e www.dolphins.gr (see also Blue Star Ferries earlier).

## Trolleybuses

Athens' overhead cable trolley-buses run between 5am-midnight. EOT's free map shows most of the routes.

A flat fare of €0.44 covers a one-way journey on buses and trolleys. Purchase tickets at a transport kiosk or at most *periptera* (kiosks). Validate tickets onboard by inserting them in the orange machines placed throughout the vehicle.

## Taxi

Athens' taxis are inexpensive but hailing one can be incredibly frustrating. During busy times, you may have to stand on the pavement and shout your destination as they pass (and they don't always slow down). If a taxi is going your way, the driver may stop even if there are already passengers inside, but this does not mean you share the fare. Check the meter when you get in,

deduct that amount from the final fare and add the flagfall.

Flagfall is €0.73, with surcharges from ports, railway and bus stations (€0.47), the airport (€0.88) and for baggage (€0.16 per item over 10kg). The day rate (€0.22 per km) doubles between midnight-5am (tariff 2). A minimum fare of €1.47 applies.

You can also call a radio taxi (€2.05 extra). Radio taxis in central Athens include: Athina 1 (☎ 01 0921 7942), Evropi (☎ 01 0502 9764), Ikaros (☎ 01 0515 2800) and Kosmos (☎ 1300).

## Car & Motorcycle

Driving in Athens can be quite daunting and frustrating. Roads are not always well signposted and you don't get much notice of when to turn or change lanes. Unless you're familiar with the city, one-way streets and no-through roads can leave you stranded or going around in circles.

### Road Rules

Someone once said red lights in Athens were merely a suggestion and this sums up the traffic chaos that can reign in the centre. There are road rules – and sometimes they are even enforced. Athenian's creative parking skills are legendary. Greeks drive on the right. Seatbelts are compulsory but few people wear them in the front, let alone back-seat passengers. The minimum driving age is 18 years. The speed limit in retail and residential areas is 40km/h and 120km/h on highways and motorways. The blood alcohol limit is 0.05%.

### Rental

Car rentals are expensive but you really only need one for excursions out of Athens. Multinationals can charge up to 25% more than local companies. The top of Syngrou, off Amalias, is lined with car-rental firms, including Avis (☎ 01 0322 4951), Budget (☎ 01 0921 4771), Europcar (☎ 01 0924 8810), Hertz (☎ 01 0922 0102) and Sixt (☎ 01 0922 0171).

Peak-season weekly rates with unlimited mileage and minimum insurance start at about €369.77 (add extra for 18% VAT and optional extras, such as collision damage, theft waivers and personal accident insurance).

### Driving Licence & Permit
A valid license from your home country should suffice, but some insurance policies require an international driving permit.

### Motoring Organisations
The Greek Automobile Club (ELPA; Athens Tower, Messogion 2-4; ☎ 01 0779 1615) has a toll-free 24hr emergency number (☎ 104) if your vehicle breaks down. The club offers reciprocal services to members of national automobile associations with a valid membership card.

# PRACTICAL INFORMATION

## Climate & When to Go

Spring and late autumn are the best times to visit. It is pleasantly warm and sunny, the archaeological sites and museums are less crowded, and hotel rooms are easier to find – and cheaper.

Winter is generally mild and sunny compared to other European capitals but there is the occasional rainy day (and in 2001 it even snowed!). Accommodation is at its cheapest, with some excellent deals.

In summer, particularly during July and August heatwaves, the temperatures can hover around 40°C for days on end. Most Athenians escape to the islands, making it easier to get around. Hotel rooms are expensive and hard to find.

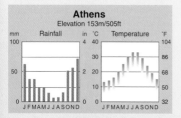

## Tourist Information

### Tourist Information Abroad
Information on Athens is available from the Greek National Tourist Organisation (GNTO; e www.gnto.gr), referred to as EOT in Greece.

Australia & New Zealand
   51 Pitt St, Sydney NSW 2000
   (☎ 02-9241 1663-5)

Canada
   1300 Bay St, Main Level, Toronto, Ontario M5R 3K8
   (☎ 416-968 2220)

Japan
   Fukuda Bldg West, 5F 2-11-3 Akasaka Minato-Ku, Tokyo 107
   (☎ 813-3505 5917)

UK & Ireland
   4 Conduit St, London W1R
   (☎ 207-7734 5997)

USA
   *New York*: Olympic Tower, 645 5th Ave, New York, NY 10022
   (☎ 212-421 5777)
   *Los Angeles*: Suite 2198, 611 W 6th St, Los Angeles, CA 92668
   (☎ 213-626 6696)

## Local Tourist Information

The GNTO (EOT) has multilingual staff and information on all aspects of the city, including various maps, travel brochures, public transport and ferry timetables and assistance with hotel bookings. The Tourist Police have a 24hr tourist information hotline on ☎ 171. Some EOT branches include:

EOT Information
Amerikis 2, Syntagma (7, H6; ☎ 01 0331 0565, 01 0331 0562; Mon-Fri 9am-4.30pm)

Eleftherios Venizelos Airport,
Arrivals Terminal (1, D5; ☎ 01 0353 0445-7; daily 8am-10pm)

Piraeus
EOT Bldg, 1st Fl, Marina Zea (5, E6; ☎ 01 0452 2591, 01 0452 2586)

# Embassies & Consulates

Australia
D. Soutsou 37, Ambelokipi (6, A8; ☎ 01 0645 0404)

Canada
Ioanna Genadiou 4, Evangelismos (6, D6; ☎ 01 0727 3400)

Japan
Vasilissis Sofias 64, Ambelokipi (6, D7; ☎ 01 0723 3732)

New Zealand
Kifissias 268, Halandri (1, C4; ☎ 01 0687 4701)

South Africa
Kifissias 60, Maroussi (1, B4; ☎ 01 0680 6656/7)

UK
Ploutarhou 1, Kolonaki (6, E4; ☎ 01 0727 2600)

USA
Vasilissis Sofias 91, Ambelokipi (6, C8; ☎ 01 0721 2951)

# Money

## Currency

Greece adopted the single European Union (EU) currency, the euro (pronounced 'evro' in Greek) on 1 Jan 2002. The drachma was completely phased out by 1 Mar 2002. The prices in this book are conversions from drachma and may change slightly.

### Drachma – Euro Conversion

| Dr | € | Dr | € |
| --- | --- | --- | --- |
| 340.75 | 1.00 | 8518.75 | 25 |
| 511.13 | 1.50 | 17037.75 | 50 |
| 681.50 | 2.00 | 34075.00 | 100 |
| 851.88 | 2.50 | 51112.50 | 150 |
| 1703.75 | 5.00 | 68150.00 | 200 |
| 3407.50 | 10.00 | 170375.00 | 500 |
| 6815.00 | 20.00 | 340750.00 | 1000 |

## Travellers Cheques

American Express, Visa, Thomas Cook and Euro-cheques are widely accepted and have efficient replacement policies but cannot be used as hard currency. You can cash travellers cheques in all banks, exchange bureaus and big hotels. American Express (☎ 01 0322 3380), at Ermou 7 Syntagma, charges no commission. It's open Mon-Fri 8am-4pm and Sat 8.30am-1.30pm. Have your passport with you, as ID is necessary.

## Credit Cards

Plastic is accepted in most hotels, retail stores, travel- and car-rental agencies, but not in all restaurants. Many retailers will give you better discounts if you pay cash. The most widely accepted cards are American Express, Diners, MasterCard and Visa. For assistance or to report lost or stolen cards call:

American Express ☎ 01 0324 4975-9,
(toll-free) ☎ 00 800 44 122296
Diners Club ☎ 01 0929 1030

MasterCard/Eurocard
☎ 01 0950 3600, 01 0929 0100
Visa International
☎ 00 800 11 638 0304 (toll-free)

## ATMs

Automatic Teller Machines are everywhere in Athens, with most operating in several languages. Cirrus, Plus and Maestro users can also make withdrawals all over town. Some of the banks around Syntagma also have Automatic Foreign Exchange Machines that take all major European currencies, Australian and US dollars and Japanese yen.

## Changing Money

Licensed foreign exchange bureaus can be found around Omonia and Syntagma. Shop around but banks usually offer the most competitive rates.

Banking hrs are Mon-Thurs 8am-2pm and Fri 8am-1.30pm. The National Bank of Greece (☎ 01 0334 0500) at Karageorgi Servias 6 Syntagma is also open Mon-Fri 3.30-6.30pm, Sat 9am-3pm and Sun 9am-1pm. Eurochange is open 8am-9pm (Karageorgi Servias 2, Syntagma ☎ 01 0331 2462; Filellinon 22, Plaka, ☎ 01 0324 3997 & Omonias 10, Plateia Omonia; ☎ 01 0523 4816).

## Tipping

Tipping is customary but not compulsory. In restaurants, the service charge is included in the bill, but most people still leave a small tip or at least round off the bill. This applies to taxis as well – a small tip for good service is much appreciated.

## Discounts

Children under 18 and seniors over 65 get discounts at most museums and ancient sites, and sometimes get free admission into state-run museums. Families can also get discounts at some museums and galleries. Some private airlines, such as Cronus, offer discount fares to seniors over 65. Children under 12 pay up to 50% less with some tour companies.

## Student & Youth Cards

Students with an International Student Identity Card (ISIC) should not have a problem obtaining discounts to archaeological sites, museums, cinemas and public transport. EU students get free admission to many museums and archaeological sites. Discounts may also apply for domestic and EU flights.

## Seniors' Cards

Card-carrying EU pensioners can claim a range of different benefits, such as reduced admission charges to museums, cinemas, theatres and ancient sites, as well as discounts on public transport. Others should declare their status upfront.

## Travel Insurance

A policy covering theft, loss, medical expenses and compensation for cancellation or delays in your travel arrangements is highly recommended when travelling anywhere. If items are lost or stolen, make sure you get a police report straight away, otherwise your insurer might not pay up.

## Opening Hours

Shops
Tues, Thurs & Fri 9am-2pm & 5.30-8.30pm (winter: 5-8pm); Mon, Wed & Sat 9am-3pm

Banks
Mon-Thurs 8am-2pm, Fri 8am-1.30pm

Department Stores & Supermarkets
Mon-Fri 8am-8pm, Sat 8am-3pm

Kiosks *(periptera)*
Open early morning until late, with 24hr kiosks in some locations especially in areas around Syntagma and Omonia

## Public Holidays

All banks, shops and most museums and ancient sites close on public holidays. See page 89 in the Entertainment chapter for information on special events around Athens and Greece.

| | |
|---|---|
| Jan 1 | New Year's Day |
| Jan 6 | Epiphany |
| Feb/Mar | Ash Monday |
| Mar 25 | Greek Independence Day |
| Mar/Apr | Good Friday |
| Mar/Apr | (Orthodox) Easter Sunday |
| May 1 | Labour Day/Spring Festival |
| Jun 4 | Agios Pnevmatos |
| Aug 15 | Feast of the Assumption of the Virgin |
| Oct 28 | Ohi Day |
| Dec 25 | Christmas Day |
| Dec 26 | Agios Stephanos |

## Time

Athens is 2hrs ahead of GMT, 1hr ahead of Central European Time and 7hrs ahead of Eastern Standard Time. Daylight-savings is in effect from the last Sunday in March to the last Sunday in October. At noon in Athens it's:

5am in New York
2am in Los Angeles
10am in London
noon in Johannesburg
8pm in Sydney
10pm in Auckland

## Electricity

Electricity is 220V AC (50Hz). Plugs are the standard continental type with two round pins. Appliances from North America require a transformer and British and Australian ones need an adaptor.

## Weights & Measures

The metric system is standard. Like other Europeans, Greeks use commas in decimals and points to indicate thousands. See the conversion table on page 122.

## Post

The mail system is quite efficient these days. Unfortunately, there can still be long queues but at least you take a number. Post offices *(tahidromia)* are easily identifiable by the yellow signs. The main city post offices are at Omonia and Syntagma (see below).

### Postal Rates

Postcards and airmail letters to destinations within the EU cost €0.53/0.82 for up to 20/50g to send. Other destinations cost €0.58/0.88 for up to 20/50g. Post within the EU takes 7-8 days and 9-11 days to the USA, Australia and New Zealand. Some tourist shops also sell stamps, but with a 10% surcharge. Express mail costs an extra €1.17 and should ensure delivery in 3 days within the EU. Valuables should be sent by registered post, which costs an extra €1.03.

### Opening Hours

Most suburban post offices are open Mon-Fri 7.30am-2pm. Athens' Central Post Office on Eolou 100 (7, F5) and the one at Syntagma Square (7, K6) are open Mon-Fri 7.30am-8pm, Sat 7.30am-2pm and Sun 9am-1pm.

## Telephone

There are public phones all over in Athens. The I (information) button provides user instructions in English. All booths take phonecards, giving you a specific number of units depending on the cost of the card. Local calls cost one unit per min.

### Phonecards

All kiosks, corner shops and tourist shops sell phonecards (€2.93/5.57/12.32/24.65 for 100/200/500/1000 units) allowing domestic and international calls.

Lonely Planet's eKno Communication Card, provides competitive international calls (although you should avoid using it for local calls), messaging services and free email for travellers. Visit the eKno website at ⓔ www.ekno.lonelyplanet .com for details on joining and accessing this service.

### Mobile Phones

Greece uses the same GSM system as most EU countries, Asia and Australia. Check that your service provider offers international roaming. The main mobile phone providers are Panafon, Telestet and CosmOTE.

North America and Japan use a cellular phone system that is incompatible with Europe. Phones can be rented from some hotels as well as Euroline (☎ 01 0985 9990) and Rent-a-phone (☎ 01 0931 9951).

### Country & City Codes

| | |
|---|---|
| Greece | ☎ 30 |
| Athens | ☎ 10 |

### New Telephone Numbers

A new 10-digit phone system for fixed and mobile phones has been introduced in Greece. The changes are taking place in several phases. The numbers in this guide will be correct until Oct 2002.

After Oct 2002, you will have to substitute the 01 prefix for Athens fixed lines with a 21 prefix and the 0 in mobiles with a 6. Refer to the table below as a reference to these changes.

### Useful Numbers

| | |
|---|---|
| Local Directory Inquiries | ☎ 131 |
| International Directory Inquiries | ☎ 161, 162 |
| Domestic Operator | ☎ 151, 152 |
| International Operator | ☎ 161 |
| Reverse-Charge (collect) | ☎ 161 |

### International Direct Dial Codes

Dial ☎ 00 followed by:

| | |
|---|---|
| Australia | ☎ 61 |
| Canada | ☎ 1 |
| Japan | ☎ 81 |
| New Zealand | ☎ 64 |
| South Africa | ☎ 27 |
| UK | ☎ 44 |
| USA | ☎ 1 |

## Digital Resources

There are plenty of Internet cafes in Athens, charging average hourly rates of €2.93-5.86 and offering the

### Telephone Number Changes

| Call | Local | From Abroad to Athens | Mobile call from Athens |
|---|---|---|---|
| Old number | ☎ 123 4567 | ☎ +301 123 4567 | ☎ 093 123 4567 |
| Jan-Sept 2002 | ☎ 010 123 4567 | ☎ +30 10 123 4567 | ☎ 093 123 4567 |
| From Oct 2002 | ☎ 210 123 4567 | ☎ +30 21 123 4567 | ☎ 693 123 4567 |

usual range of computer services. Business centres, such as those at the airport, have great facilities but charge about double what you would pay at Internet cafes. A few monitors are set up at the airport allowing free access, but tend to attract long queues.

### Internet Service Providers

The vast majority of global ISPs have dial-in nodes in Greece. It's best to download this information from their sites before you leave home. Greece's main ISP providers are Otenet, Forthnet, and Hellas Online, however they usually require at least a one-month contract. Compulink's e-free start-up (☎ 08 003 999 toll-free) pack gets you online immediately with 30hrs of online time for €9.99.

### Internet Cafes

If you can't access the Internet from where you're staying (or it's too expensive), head to an Internet cafe:

Ivis Internet Services
   Mitropoleos 3, Syntagma (9, E9; ☎ 01 0324 3365; e ivis@travelling.gr; daily 8.30-12.30am; €1.17/15mins)

Museum Internet Cafe
   Patission 46 (7, C5; ☎ 01 0883 3418; e www.museumcafe.gr; daily 9-3am; €1.47/20mins)

Plaka Internet World
   Pandrossou 29, Plaka (9, D4; ☎ 01 0331 6056; e plakaworld@internet.gr; daily 10am-11pm ; €1.47/15mins)

webcafe
   George 10, Plateia Kaningos, Omonia (7, E5; ☎ 01 0330 3063; Mon-Sat 9am-2am, Sun 11-2am; €2.05/30mins)

### Useful Sites

The Lonely Planet Web site (e www.lonelyplanet.com) offers a speedy link to many Greek Web sites. Others to try include:

Go Greece
   e www.gogreece.gr

Greece Now
   e www.greece.gr

Hellas Online
   e www.hol.gr/greece

Ministry of Culture
   e www.culture.gr

## Doing Business

Most major hotels have business centres with fax, photocopying, Internet access and other services. International Business Services provides for the needs of executives and business travellers, including translation services (Mihalakopoulou 29; ☎ 01 0724 5541; fax 01 0724 950).

Useful organisations include the Hellenic Centre for Investment (ELKE; Mitropoleos 3; ☎ 01 0324 2070; fax 010 324 2079; e www.elke.gr) which provides various free services, and the Athens Chamber of Commerce and Industry (Akadimias 7; ☎ 01 0360 4815; fax 01 0361 6408; e www.acci.gr).

## Newspapers & Magazines

Greeks are avid newsreaders as the 15 daily newspapers confirm. The weekly *Athinorama* entertainment magazine covers events, cinema, theatre, bars and other activities in Greek but its Web site (e www.athinorama.gr) has a limited English search facility.

The biggest selection of foreign press publications can be found at the 24hr kiosks in Omonia and Syntagma, and in Kolonaki.

The only daily news in English (except Sunday) is the eight-page

edition of *Kathimerini* (**e** www
.kathimerini.gr) in English, published with the *International Herald Tribune*. The weekly *Athens
News* (**e** www.athensnews.gr) carries Greek and international news
and features. Both publications
print movie and entertainment
listings.

An excellent English publication
on Greece is the bimonthly *Odyssey*
(**e** www.odyssey.gr) magazine, a
glossy which also publishes a handy
annual summer guide to Athens
and Greece.

## Radio

Athens has more than 20 radio stations playing everything from hip-
hop to Greek folk music.

The state-owned ERA 1 and 2
(91.6FM and 93.6FM) play pop and
rock; ERA 3 (95.6FM) plays classical
music.

Galaxy (92.0FM) airs CNN news
briefs along with foreign pop,
while Flash (91.6FM) has daily
English news bulletins at 9am, 3pm
and 8pm. Turn to Village 88FM
(88.0FM) for the latest in music,
Radio Gold (105FM) for all things
retro, Kiss FM (90.9FM) for a mix of
rock and techno and Nitro (108.2FM)
which plays various alternative
rock; Ciao (104.2FM) for Greek
pop or Melodia (100FM) for Greek
nostalgia.

## TV

Greece has several private TV chan-
nels but most are very ordinary.
Channel surfing might get you a
movie in English or some old
episodes of your favourite US
soaps. The state-run ET 1, ET 3 and
NET have quality programs, docu-
mentaries and news in Greek.
Cable TV is available but not widespread.

## Photography & Video

Most major brands and types of
film are available, as are black-and-
white film, slide film and camera
gear and repairs. Developing a roll
of 36 single exposures costs about
€7.33.

Greece uses the PAL video system, which is incompatible with
the North American and Japanese
NTSC and the French Secam, unless
you have a multisystem machine.

## Health

### Immunisations

No vaccinations are required for
entry into Greece. A yellow fever
vaccination certificate is required if
you are coming from an infected
area. Routine inoculations for
Tetanus and Diptheria, Polio and
Hepatitis A are generally recommended.

### Precautions

Health conditions in Athens are
generally excellent and tap water
is drinkable. Since the scare with
mad cow disease in Europe, many
restaurants have taken beef off the
menu as a precautionary measure.
The heat in summer can be stifling,
so drink plenty of water to avoid
dehydration and heat exhaustion
and wear sunscreen, sensible light
clothing and a hat.

Like anywhere else, practise the
usual precautions when it comes to
safe sex; condoms are available at
pharmacies and supermarkets.

### Insurance & Medical
Treatment

Travel insurance is advisable to
cover any medical treatment you
may need. Athens' chaotic and
under-funded public hospitals can
be quite unpleasant. While the
standard of medical care is adequate and professional expertise

high, hygiene, nursing care and general comforts are not. Private medical treatment is much better, but expensive. Emergency treatment in public hospitals is available free to all nationalities.

## Medical Services

Accident and emergency treatment is available 24hrs at duty hospitals, which operate on a roster basis. Dial ☎ 106 for information about the nearest emergency hospital or check the listings in the daily *IHT/Kathimerini* or *Athens News*. A round-the-clock service is provided by SOS-Doctors, who charge a fixed rate for hotel or home visits, but they do accept credit cards (☎ 1016).

Major hospitals include:

Evangelismos (Public)
Ipsilantou 45-47, Kolonaki (6, D5; ☎ 01 0720 1000)

Athens Euroclinic (Private)
Athanasiadou 9, Ambelokipi (6, A9; ☎ 01 0641 6600; 1011 emergencies)

Agia Sofia (Children's Public Hospital)
Thivon & Mikras Asias, Goudi (6, B10; ☎ 01 0746 7000)

## Dental Services

If you chip a tooth or require emergency treatment it's best to ask at your hotel or contact your embassy. Minor procedures will require cash, but if you have travel insurance you will be able to claim any expenses when you get home.

## Pharmacies

Athens' pharmacists are well trained and are licensed to dispense a wide range of medicines that in other countries can only be prescribed by a doctor. Most of the ones around Syntagma Square have staff that can speak at least some English. A monthly schedule of after-hrs duty pharmacies is posted on pharmacy doors, while the *IHT/Kathimerini* and *Athens News* publish daily lists. The airport has the only permanent 24-hr pharmacy.

## Toilets

Public toilets are rare in Athens, so head to fast food places like McDonald's. If you really get stuck, most restaurants will allow you to use their restrooms if you ask politely. Don't forget that those little bins in all toilets are for paper waste, so never flush toilet paper down the toilet. What might seem quirky helps avoid clogging the system.

## Safety Concerns

Athens is a very safe city and violent crime aimed at tourists is rare. Walking around Plaka and the historic centre is usually safe. Even in the winter there is bustle and activity. It's always safer to keep handbags slung across your chest and avoid keeping a lot of cash and valuables on you, as there are pickpockets in busy areas. Many Roma (gypsies) and beggars go around selling anything from tissues to flowers, or singing on trains to elicit 'donations'. Apart from the frustration of being interrupted over lunch or dinner, they don't pose much of a real threat.

### Lost Property

The best course of action is to call the 24-hr tourist police number (☎ 171) and explain where you lost your property. They can refer you to the appropriate department.

### Keeping Copies

Make photocopies of all your important documents, keep some with you separate from the originals and leave a copy at home. You can also store details of documents in Lonely Planet's free online Travel Vault, password-protected and accessible worldwide. See e www.ekno.lonelyplanet.com.

## Emergency Numbers

There's a toll-free, 24hr emergency assistance number (☎ 112; English or French) for visitors. Other numbers include:

| | |
|---|---|
| Ambulance | ☎ 166 |
| Fire | ☎ 199 |
| Police | ☎ 100 |

## Women Travellers

Greek men had a notorious reputation for pestering women, especially foreigners, but the practice (more of a nuisance than an actual threat) is far less prevalent now. Taxi drivers are usually respectful, even if grumpy. However, it is always wise to avoid walking in deserted parts of the city and parks at night and to use common sense.

Items for personal and sanitary hygiene are widely available in supermarkets and pharmacies. Contraceptives are sold over the counter.

## Gay & Lesbian Travellers

Homosexuality is generally frowned upon, but there is tolerance of gays and lesbians. The local gay community is not very visible, although a significant closet culture exists. It would be wise not to be openly affectionate in public unless you are in a dedicated gay venue.

That said, Athens has a busy gay bar scene, centred mostly around Makrigianni, south of the Temple of Olympian Zeus.

### Information & Organisations

There's basic information for travellers on the Inertnet at: e www.geocities.com/WestHollywood/2225/index.html, www.jwpublishing.com/gayscape/menugreece.html or you can check out the Spartacus gay travel guide.

## Senior Travellers

Narrow streets, cobbled pathways and badly made footpaths can make it hard for senior travellers. Archaeological sites can be particularly hard going. But seniors are usually treated with respect, especially on public transport, where it's the 'norm' to offer seats to older travellers.

## Disabled Travellers

Provision of facilities for the mobility impaired is a recent phenomenon, being fast-tracked for the Paralympics in 2004.

Many museums have stairs, most archaeological sites are not wheelchair friendly and public transport can be fairly crowded. Modern restaurants may have restrooms that allow easier access, but most tavernas and inner-city eateries tend to have toilets down stairs.

Hotels are upgrading their facilities and quite a few of the better ones are well equipped.

Newer buses and trolleys are wider and have seats assigned for those with disabilities, but getting on or off is not easy. The new metro has lifts to the platforms. The airport has excellent facilities.

### Information & Organisations

The Panhellenic Union of Paraplegic & Physically Challenged (Dimitsanis 3-5, Moschato; ☎ 01 0483 2564; e www.pasipka.gr) can provide some information.

# Language

The official language is Greek, but a big percentage of the population, particularly young people, speak English.

Greek is probably the oldest of all European languages, with an oral tradition dating back 4000 years and a written tradition of approximately 3000 years. Modern Greek developed from a number of regional dialects, predominantly from the south. Greek is written using its own distinctive 24-letter alphabet, from which the Russian Cyrillic alphabet and its many variants were based. Transliterations into the Roman alphabet are used in this guide; note that the letter combination **dh** is pronounced as the 'th' in 'them'.

## Basics

| | |
|---|---|
| Hello. | yasas |
| | yasu (informal) |
| Goodbye. | andio |
| Good morning. | kalimera |
| Good afternoon. | herete |
| Good evening. | kalispera |
| Please. | parakalo |
| Thank you. | efharisto |
| Yes. | ne |
| No. | ohi |
| Sorry. (excuse me, forgive me) | sighnomi |
| How are you? | ti kanete? |
| | ti kanis? (informal) |
| I'm well, thanks. | kala efharisto |
| Do you speak English? | milate anglika? |
| I understand. | katalaveno |
| I don't understand. | dhen katalaveno |
| Where is ...? | pou ine ...? |
| How much? | poso kani? |
| When? | pote? |

## Getting Around

| | |
|---|---|
| What time does the ... leave/arrive? | ti ora fevyil ftani to ...? |
| boat | karavi |
| train | treno |
| I'd like a return ticket. | tha ithela isitirio me epistrofi |
| metro station | metro stathmos |
| How do I get to ...? | pos tha pao sto/sti ...? |
| Where is ...? | pou ine ...? |
| Is it far? | ine makria? |

## Accommodation

| | |
|---|---|
| I'd like a ... | thelo ena ... |
| single | mono |
| double | dhiplo |
| room with bathroom | dhomatio me banio |

## Around Town

| | |
|---|---|
| I'm looking for (the) ... | psahno ya ... |
| bank | tin trapeza |
| beach | tin paralia |
| kiosk | to periptero |
| market | tin aghora |
| museum | to musio |
| ruins | ta arhaia |

## Time, Days & Numbers

| | |
|---|---|
| What time is it? | ti ora ine? |
| It's ... | ine ... |
| today | simera |
| tonight | apopse |
| now | tora |
| yesterday | hthes |
| tomorrow | avrio |
| Sunday | kyriaki |
| Monday | dheftera |
| Tuesday | triti |
| Wednesday | tetarti |
| Thursday | pempti |
| Friday | paraskevi |
| Saturday | savato |

| | | | |
|---|---|---|---|
| 0 | midhen | 5 | pende |
| 1 | enas (m) | 6 | exi |
| | mia (f) | 7 | epta |
| | ena (n) | 8 | ohto |
| 2 | dhio | 9 | enea |
| 3 | tris (m & f) | 10 | dheka |
| | tria (n) | 100 | ekato |
| 4 | teseris (m & f) | 1000 | hilii (m) |
| | tesera (n) | | hilies (f) |
| | | | hilia (n) |

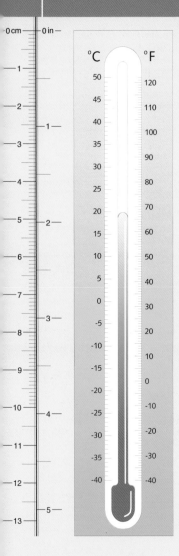

## Conversion Table

### Clothing Sizes
*Measurements approximate only; try before you buy.*

#### Women's Clothing

| | | | | | | |
|---|---|---|---|---|---|---|
| Aust/NZ | 8 | 10 | 12 | 14 | 16 | 18 |
| Europe | 36 | 38 | 40 | 42 | 44 | 46 |
| Japan | 5 | 7 | 9 | 11 | 13 | 15 |
| UK | 8 | 10 | 12 | 14 | 16 | 18 |
| USA | 6 | 8 | 10 | 12 | 14 | 16 |

#### Women's Shoes

| | | | | | | |
|---|---|---|---|---|---|---|
| Aust/NZ | 5 | 6 | 7 | 8 | 9 | 10 |
| Europe | 35 | 36 | 37 | 38 | 39 | 40 |
| France only | 35 | 36 | 38 | 39 | 40 | 42 |
| Japan | 22 | 23 | 24 | 25 | 26 | 27 |
| UK | 3½ | 4½ | 5½ | 6½ | 7½ | 8½ |
| USA | 5 | 6 | 7 | 8 | 9 | 10 |

#### Men's Clothing

| | | | | | | |
|---|---|---|---|---|---|---|
| Aust/NZ | 92 | 96 | 100 | 104 | 108 | 112 |
| Europe | 46 | 48 | 50 | 52 | 54 | 56 |
| Japan | S | | M | M | | L |
| UK | 35 | 36 | 37 | 38 | 39 | 40 |
| USA | 35 | 36 | 37 | 38 | 39 | 40 |

#### Men's Shirts (Collar Sizes)

| | | | | | | |
|---|---|---|---|---|---|---|
| Aust/NZ | 38 | 39 | 40 | 41 | 42 | 43 |
| Europe | 38 | 39 | 40 | 41 | 42 | 43 |
| Japan | 38 | 39 | 40 | 41 | 42 | 43 |
| UK | 15 | 15½ | 16 | 16½ | 17 | 17½ |
| USA | 15 | 15½ | 16 | 16½ | 17 | 17½ |

#### Men's Shoes

| | | | | | | |
|---|---|---|---|---|---|---|
| Aust/NZ | 7 | 8 | 9 | 10 | 11 | 12 |
| Europe | 41 | 42 | 43 | 44½ | 46 | 47 |
| Japan | 26 | 27 | 27.5 | 28 | 29 | 30 |
| UK | 7 | 8 | 9 | 10 | 11 | 12 |
| USA | 7½ | 8½ | 9½ | 10½ | 11½ | 12½ |

## Weights & Measures

### Weight
1kg = 2.2lb
1lb = 0.45kg
1g = 0.04oz
1oz = 28g

### Volume
1 litre = 0.26 US gallons
1 US gallon = 3.8 litres
1 litre = 0.22 imperial gallons
1 imperial gallon = 4.55 litres

### Length & Distance
1 inch = 2.54cm
1cm = 0.39 inches
1m = 3.3ft = 1.1yds
1ft = 0.3m
1km = 0.62 miles
1 mile = 1.6km

# lonely planet

Lonely Planet is the world's most successful independent travel information company with offices in Australia, the US, UK and France. With a reputation for comprehensive, reliable travel information, Lonely Planet is a print and electronic publishing leader, with over 650 titles and 22 series catering for travellers' individual needs.

At Lonely Planet we believe that travellers can make a positive contribution to the countries they visit – if they respect their host communities and spend their money wisely. Since 1986 a percentage of the income from books has been donated to aid and human rights projects.

## www.lonelyplanet.com

For news, views and free subscriptions to print and email newsletters, and a full list of LP titles, click on Lonely Planet's award-winning website.

## On the Town

A romantic escape to Paris or a mad shopping dash through New York City, the locals' secret bars or a city's top attractions – whether you have 24 hours to kill or months to explore, Lonely Planet's On the Town products will give you the low-down.

**Condensed guides** are ideal pocket guides for when time is tight. Their quick-view maps, full-colour layout and opinionated reviews help short-term visitors target the top sights and discover the very best eating, shopping and entertainment options a city has to offer.

For more indepth coverage, **City guides** offer insights into a city's character and cultural background as well as providing broad coverage of where to eat, stay and play. **CitySync**, a digital guide for your handheld unit, allows you to reference stacks of opinionated, well-researched travel information. Portable and durable **City Maps** are perfect for locating those back-street bars or hard-to-find local haunts.

*'Ideal for a generation of fast movers.'*

– *Gourmet Traveller* on Condensed guides

## Condensed Guides

- Amsterdam
- Barcelona
- Boston
- Bangkok (Sept 2002)
- California
- Chicago
- Crete
- Dublin
- Frankfurt
- Hong Kong
- Los Angeles (Oct 2002)
- London
- New York City
- Paris
- Prague
- Rome
- San Francisco (Oct 2002)
- Singapore (Oct 2002)
- Sydney
- Tokyo
- Venice
- Washington, DC

# index

*See also separate indexes for Places to Eat (p. 126), Places to Stay (p. 127), Shops (p. 127) and Sights with map references (p. 128).*

# PLACES TO EAT